STATE of the
NANNY

STATE of the NANNY
Telling it like it really is

LOUISE DUNHAM

MONTEREY PRESS

First published in 2017
by Monterey Press
7 Westbourne St
Brunswick VIC 3056
Australia
www.montereypress.com

Copyright © Louise Dunham, 2017

Website: www.placementsolutions.com.au

All rights reserved. No part of this publication may be reproduced, stored in a retrieval system or transmitted in any form by any means, electronic, mechanical, photocopying, recording or otherwise, without the prior written permission of the publishers and copyright holders.

Louise Dunham asserts the moral right to be identified as the author of this work.

Cover artwork by David Brewster
Designed and typeset by Lu Sexton

National Library of Australia
Cataloguing-in-Publication entry

Creator: Dunham, Louise, 1953-.

Title: State of the nanny: Telling it like it really is / by Louise Dunham.

ISBN: 9780994429353 (paperback)

Subjects: Nannies—Australia.
          Nannies—Employment.
          Child care—Australia.
          Parent and child.

*This book could only ever be for my parents,
Anne and Ross Dunham, my daughters,
Caitlin and Sianan, and my grandson, Reuben.*

Acknowledgements

It all started with my parents, Anne and Ross Dunham, whom I have to thank for teaching me right from wrong and what are now called my 'core values' of integrity, honesty and a fair wage for all.

Then there are all the great, professional, committed nannies I have known and worked with in Australia and around the world over many years. You know who you are.

The team in my office who provide such tremendous support and who just 'get it' – that nannying is always about the children first – thank you.

I have been influenced over the years by a number of great agencies who, like me, are always pursuing a better deal for nannies and, by extension, the children they care for. I have the International Nanny Association (INA), Association of Premier Nanny Agencies (APNA) and Australian Home Care Association (ACHA) to thank here too, for their support and for 'staying the course' with their recommended practices.

I would also like to thank Kathy Harrison Webb, Susan Tokayer, Kellie Geres, Tonya Sakowicz, Daryl Camarillo, Denise Collins, Jacalyn Burke, Judy Appleton and Sue Downey. You all truly make a difference.

Lastly I want to thank our incredibly professional and enthusiastic Placement Solutions Nannies of the Year, Clare Carlisle Stranger (2014/15) and Cecily Laing (2016/17).

Contents

Foreword	xi
Introduction	1

1. It starts with fair wages & conditions — 7
- Tattered remnants — 9
- A cautionary tale — 14
- An uneven playing field, with plenty of risk all around — 17
- And about time too — 20

2. The nannying industry: heading in the right direction? — 25
- The more things change … — 27
- Increasing professionalism — 29
- 'Wot's in a name,' she sez? — 34
- The importance of ethical and moral leadership — 38
- Remembering the 'care' in child care — 43

3. Trends in child care — 47
- Getting back to 'good enough' parenting — 50
- Loosen up and build resilience — 53
- The power of learning a musical instrument — 56
- A simple truth: they want time with you — 58
- The role of the modern grandparent — 61
- It's not all black and white: welcome progress in perinatal depression — 64

4. The role of today's nanny — 67
- The many faces of the nanny — 71
- Putting the child first — 76
- Child protection — 79
- Continuing self-improvement — 81
- The 10 habits of great nannies — 83

5. The role of the parent — 87
- What to remember when hiring a nanny — 90
- Choosing an agency — 94
- How to keep your great nanny — 97
- Managing live-in and long-term nannies — 99
- Jealousy and the nanny — 101
- Dealing with the nanny moving on — 104

6. Reflections on our agency — 107
- Why we insist on face-to-face interviews with all our applicants — 110
- The question of fees — 113
- Finding other ways to care — 116
- Recognising achievement — 120
- Taking the lead on issues that matter — 123
- Continued growth — 126

The final word — 129
About the author — 133

FOREWORD

I first met Louise Dunham in 2010 at an International Nanny Association (INA) conference in San Francisco. This was Louise's first INA event and we immediately recognised kindred spirits – professionals who are passionate about quality in-home childcare and the legal and ethical treatment of nannies by families and agencies.

Louise and I served together on the board of directors of the International Nanny Association for five years. I can assure you that Louise walks the talk – she backs up her opinions (which she is always willing to share) with action. In her role as Ethics Chair, Louise insisted that ethical matters be addressed head on, in the right way, even when it wasn't always the easiest or popular course. I am proud to call her both colleague and friend.

State of the Nanny covers a lot of ground and addresses the good, the bad and the ugly in the nanny world. Louise is a natural storyteller, and her anecdotes humanise her core messages – nannying is about the children, a nanny is ethically required to put the children first, and a family or agency employer has a responsibility to do the right things regarding working conditions, fair pay and proper adherence to tax and insurance obligations.

Louise properly points out that the nanny career has come a long way from its roots in servitude. A quarter of a century ago the majority of nannies were young women earning money to pay for education or travel, and saw their nanny jobs as a temporary stop on their way to their 'real' jobs and careers. While there certainly are nannies working worldwide today who have the same notions, there is wide recognition today that nannying *is* a real job, and it absolutely can be a career.

State of the Nanny touches on some uncomfortable subjects, such as the nanny's role as a mandated reporter for child abuse, postnatal depression and a mother's jealousy of the nanny. Louise addresses the subjects straight on with her unique combination of frankness and humor. Louise reminds the reader thoughout that the focus needs to stay on the quality of care and everyone in the industry must remain committed to doing the right thing, even when that involves more work, money or inconvenience.

Kathy Webb
Co-Founder, HomeWork Solutions Inc.
homeworksolutions.com

INTRODUCTION

In the 1990s I was involved with a Victorian government committee overseeing the implementation of the state's first Working with Children Check. As a result of that work, I got to know a number of sitting politicians. The 1999 Victorian state election saw the Liberal (Kennett) government unexpectedly thrown out of office, and soon after, a Liberal politician asked me to meet her for a coffee.

'On the night my leader was deposed,' she said, 'as if that wasn't bad enough, I went home and my husband told me he was leaving me. The next morning my nanny told me that she was leaving too [not with the husband!]. I want to tell you that I can live without my leader, and I can even live without my husband ... but I cannot live or do my job without my nanny.'

With that she asked me to find her a replacement nanny as soon as I could.

This interchange was as clear a message as I've ever had about the importance of nannies in the lives of those who hire them and in the lives of the children the nannies care for.

I've been working in the nanny industry for just under 30 years, a period in which organised child care, both inside and outside the home, has been through many ups and downs, and changed enormously. Much has changed for the better, but there is still plenty of room for improvement and it is very important that we continue to seek that improvement. That requires people who have informed opinions to speak out, and anyone who knows me knows that as well as my long experience in the industry, I'm rarely short of an opinion. This book is one way of expressing my opinions, which is why I've written it.

When I reflect on the last 30 years, we are not as far along as I would have hoped. Progress is slow in a number of areas. With each change of federal or state government we get incremental change, but rarely anything bold. Sometimes there is a step back rather than forward. In some cases governments will create or clarify the laws – such as the requirement that nannies cannot operate as independent contractors – but then do little or nothing to implement those laws in practice. (More on that later.)

We have made some good ground in building the 'professional' status of nannies, though there is still an awfully long road to travel on that issue. There is still not the necessary level of respect, support and understanding for the challenges that nannies face, the level of responsibility they take on and the fact that they earn their money and should be paid accordingly. The 'anyone can mind a child' mindset is still widespread and needs to be removed. Parents need to understand that to use untrained carers (usually in order to save money) is to compromise on their children's care, which is ultimately demeaning to the children themselves by tacitly saying that they are not important enough to be professionally cared for.

Which brings me to education and training. Professionalism will improve, along with community attitudes, provided we continue to provide quality training for nannies. There is an obligation on nannies here too. They should be expected to undergo formal education and to take up further training opportunities. Formal training really should be a requirement for anyone charged with looking after a child. This is the case in long-day care, so there is no reason why it should not also be the case for in-home care – more so, given that nannies work on their own.

This book is a call to arms on these and a number of other issues. My hope is that it will be read, discussed and debated by nannies, nanny agency operators and those who hire nannies. As the ancient Greek proverb says, 'A society grows great when old men plant trees whose shade they know they shall never sit in'. Let this book be one of those trees for the nanny industry, generating a conversation that continues long after I have retired.

1

IT STARTS WITH FAIR WAGES & CONDITIONS

Tattered remnants

After moving house in the last year or so, I realised as I unpacked that some of my belongings have been a constant – packed and unpacked, packed and unpacked – throughout all the houses I've lived in between my childhood and my 60th year.

I unpacked, again, the tattered remnants of a lace tablecloth given to me long ago by my mother, after it was passed down to her by her grandmother, Catherine (Cate) Shannon. The tablecloth is in ruins now and I don't have the skills, the time or the patience to repair it. However, I cannot throw it away. As I fondle the torn Irish lacework I think of the story passed down from my mother to me along with the cloth.

The lace cloth was handmade by an eight-year-old Cate in Cobh Harbour in Cork, Ireland. It was packed with her as a part of a marriage dowry before she was sent, alone, to New Zealand by her family in the 1870s, apparently so as to avoid the troubles of Cork that her brothers were involved in. Her family paid a small fee to access the assisted emigration scheme and Cate became a housemaid on the goldfields in Arrow Town. She could not read or write then, and through her long life she never learned to do so. At 16, while working as a parlour maid, Cate met the man who would become her husband. He was a notorious drunk and she kept working hard, but stayed poor all her life until she dropped dead at 94 ... chopping wood! My mother recalls a woman with long black hair, even in old age. She had fiery opinions and could weave a story. My mother and I inherited these skills, along with Cate's green eyes. And I have the lace remnant.

I have visited Cobh Harbour twice, both times in cold sleeting rain, and walked through the emigration museum, once with my own daughter, telling her the story of the leaving of her namesake. So many Irish, just as my great-grandmother, made that journey in the hope of finding sustenance and sanctuary across an ocean.

Domestic servitude runs on the other side of my family too. Two of my father's ancestors were British emigrants to Tasmania who became housemaids. Ann Cox arrived in Tasmania in 1858. She was a Methodist from Felthorpe in Norfolk, who came to Australia with her brother. Both could read and write, which was unusual at the time for the servant class. Ann worked as a domestic servant in Green Ponds, out of Hobart. She would go on to marry John Dunham and have 11 children.

Ann's neighbour was Augusta Harriet Shearer, who had arrived in Australia at age 15 with a group from the St Andrew's (Highland Emigration) Benevolent Society. She was also literate, and was also assigned as a domestic servant. Augusta married Alfred Redman, with whom she had nine children. Years later, after both John Dunham and Augusta Redman had died, Ann Dunham married Alfred Redman to create what must have been a fairly busy household – especially after Ann and Alfred went on to have another three children.

Over their many years of domestic work, history suggests that Cate, Ann, Augusta and their counterparts were almost certainly underpaid and exploited. Housework was regarded as humble women's work and was menial, lowly and lowly paid. They certainly did not receive any of the modern benefits such as sick leave, holiday pay and superannuation contributions towards retirement.

Reflecting on these stories it comes as no surprise to me that I've spent most of my working life in the area of domestic support and in pursuit of fair pay and conditions for those who work in the field.

Back in 1988 I was an emergency teacher at Heidelberg Technical School. The 'techs' in those days were public secondary schools catering for kids who were, generally speaking, more practical and less academic – kids destined to go into the trades rather than to university. The teaching was quite hard but the kids were okay under a few layers of bravado. When I had my first child, though, I couldn't continue teaching as I had no local family support. Instead I enrolled in a part-time diploma in genealogy, with the intention to eventually pursue that as a profession.

When my husband at the time brought home an Apple Macintosh Classic II (one of those early 'all-in-one' Macs) that his school had just replaced, I thought I might be able to make some money on the side by setting up a cleaning business, supplying modern versions of 'domestic servants' to busy families. As someone who has always hated cleaning, I figured there must be many other women who felt the same, even though this was 1988 and long before 'outsourcing' became as routine as it is today. The business grew and it wasn't long before one of my cleaning clients rang me, upset that her cleaning lady was not happy for her to leave her sleeping baby effectively in the cleaner's care while she ducked down to the shops. I explained to my client that I thought she was being unfair, as her child needed full adult attention, and she became the first of a string of people asking me to provide nannies and babysitters.

My business evolved from there (and I never did get the chance to pursue genealogy as a profession).

Today my agency, Placement Solutions, sends nannies and household managers to busy, successful and often stressed working parents. For the last 30 years this has been my life: organising, recruiting, placing, supporting and educating both parents and nannies, while also running the 'business' of my firm.

Of course the world of domestic servants is very different today from what it was in the 19th century.

Nannies in particular are now protected by legal award rates and all the entitlements that any worker can expect. Unfortunately that doesn't mean that all nannies receive these benefits. The law might be clear, but that doesn't stop debate continuing. Over and over the same questions keep coming up. Can nannies operate as independent contractors? Can a babysitter be paid cash in hand? Does a nanny agency have to pay entitlements to its staff? Are there still nannies who do not, despite the legal requirement otherwise, receive superannuation contributions, sick leave and holiday pay from their employers? Are there still nannies who are under-appreciated, exploited, paid cash in hand and with no clear job description?

I am tired of these questions. My own is: Why is this still a debate? It's time for Australian nanny agencies and people who use in-home help to grow up.

The Australian Tax Office (ATO) and Fair Work Commission

both stipulate clear requirements on rates of pay, leave entitlements including sick leave, superannuation contributions and so on. Legally, there would be almost no nannies who meet the minimum ATO requirements to operate as independent contractors. Legally, nannies cannot be paid cash in hand.

Yet there remain, still, countless employers of nannies who flout these laws because they know they'll probably get away with it. That some parents who directly employ their nannies do this is unfortunate, but not unexpected. That many nanny agencies still do this is frankly outrageous.

I sometimes wonder whether our acceptance of this sort of exploitation is a legacy of the colonial history of demeaning women's work. Before the experiences of women like Cate Shannon in New Zealand and Ann Dunham and Augusta Redman in Tasmania, female convicts were providing a free labour supply in the colonies – something that continued for 70 years. Immediately thereafter, from the early 1850s, the assisted emigration scheme that sent the likes of Cate from their homes provided a new pool of young women who were desperate to escape poverty at home and so were easy targets for poor treatment.

I am grateful that life is somewhat easier for each subsequent generation of women in my family, but I remain desirous that all life-affirming work – especially that involving the care of children and nurturing of families – is fully appreciated, and that those doing paid work in these fields are well compensated and receive all their legal entitlements.

A cautionary tale

The online world provides seemingly endless opportunities for those who dream of working for themselves. As a nanny, why work for an agency like mine when you can cut out the 'middle man'? All you need to do is put an ad on a website, at little or no cost, and find your own work. Get paid cash and you won't even need to pay tax. Easy ... yes?

Well, actually, no.

The recent experiences of a family friend of ours demonstrated all too well the risks associated with taking this 'solo' approach. Her story shows how cutting corners and bypassing 'the system' works both ways. If potential employees can cut corners, so too can potential employers, and that can lead to some very dubious, if not downright scary, situations.

Our friend – I'll call her Claire – is a university student who was out of work and was very keen to find a job. She decided to place an ad on the 'Gumtree' website, a sort of modern *Trading Post* on which you can advertise, for free, anything from a used lawn mower to your own labour.

Claire's 'Work wanted' ad began: 'I'm a 20-year-old female looking for cleaning, babysitting or waitressing work ...' In order to maximise her chances of a response, Claire included her mobile phone number in her ad, something the website recommended.

In the week or so after placing the ad, Claire received four responses.

The first was from someone who sent her a message giving her the opportunity to 'be my girl', for which she would be paid $2000 per week plus free accommodation.

The second was an offer to be a 'masseuse'. When Claire replied that she was not qualified to do this, the employer told her that she would be trained and that she would quickly get 'regular clients'. Claire asked them for their company name but they had none, nor a website or any other form of proof that they really existed.

The third offer was a little more promising, though only just. It was a text message offering bar work at $15 per hour. After Claire established that the work would involve essentially running a cocktail bar on her own – practically managing the bar – and questioned the pay rate, she was offered '$20 an hour if you wear revealing clothing'.

The fourth offer was the most dubious of all. I won't go into the details; suffice to say it involved 'working' in front of a camera for a fairly substantial fee.

Eventually Claire did get a genuine offer of cleaning work but, as she drove to the house of the client – oddly enough within the grounds of a converted prison – these previous offers made her very wary. It worked out, but so easily might not have.

This is the sort of world that 'going it alone' potentially takes you into, and it applies as much to in-home child care as to the sort of work Claire was looking for.

Nannies need to be careful about who they work for. They need to protect themselves against low pay (most cash employers pay less than the award rate), against maltreatment (there is nowhere to turn when working on your own) and against the ATO (cash-in-hand arrangements are illegal for both employer and employee). These are all the things a reputable, accredited agency provides – plus things like workers compensation insurance in case you are injured at work, holiday and sick leave, and ongoing training.

Claire has learnt her lesson. In future she will be dealing with agencies and employers who play by the rules. In her view, any potential benefit of flying solo is just not worth the risks.

An uneven playing field, with plenty of risk all around

The problem of 'underground' cash-in-hand work in the in-home childcare industry is not constrained to individuals who, like Claire, advertise their services independently. There remain numerous so-called nanny placement agencies that encourage, or at least turn a blind eye to, cash payments from employers.

Yes, the word 'underground' has fairly strong connotations of illegality, but that's precisely why I use it. For what we are talking about here is the provision of child care that is outside the law – which is, of course, what illegal means. And while some may suggest that the law is overly prescriptive and, dare I say it, characteristic of a 'nanny state', there are good reasons for the laws in this area. Not least of these is the safety of children who are being cared for.

There are essentially two main groups of nannies working illegally in Australia.

The first are those working for cash in hand, often labelled as *au pairs* or babysitters, but with nanny-type responsibilities. These usually untrained 'nannies' operate completely outside the system, essentially on a black market. The illegality of this situation should be obvious. It starts with the fact that the nanny is earning money that is not being declared to the ATO. Then there is the lack of workers compensation cover, professional liability and superannuation guarantee payments.

Nannies working under these circumstances operate with no protection. They are open to abuse, can be summarily dismissed at any time and are constantly risking prosecution by the ATO. Parents and, more importantly, children in these situations are also essentially unprotected. Parents are certainly risking a potentially awkward situation should they discover any form of misconduct on the part of their nanny. It's difficult to turn to the law for help when you have so obviously been ignoring it. They are also breaking the law themselves by hiring an employee on a cash-in-hand basis.

The second group of illegally operating nannies are those who work as contractors using their own Australian Business Number (ABN). A number of prominent agencies, along with parent employers, prefer this way of working as it leaves the onus for things like workers compensation and superannuation on the nanny. This reduces both internal bureaucracy and cost. The problem is that it is, as I've said, illegal. The ATO has very clear rules and tests relating to independent contractors in any industry. Operating as a contractor is only allowed when a person is operating a legitimate business, as defined by having multiple clients, having the ability to subcontract or delegate, being paid on the basis of a quoted price for a specific outcome, taking commercial risks, having control over when they work and don't work, and operating independently.

Very few nannies would meet these requirements, whether they are working for an agency or directly for a parent employer. In addition, nannies working under these conditions do so with the same lack of protection as those working for cash in hand.

Of course, people who employ nannies under either of these circumstances need to accept that they cannot qualify for any government rebates, that they cannot be sure that their nanny is up to date with current legal requirements of the profession, and that their nanny will not be getting any professional development.

Both cash-in-hand nannies and nannies working as contractors are often cheaper – sometimes substantially – than nannies provided through an accredited and responsible agency. This does have an effect on legitimate business operators like ourselves because it creates a playing field that is anything but level. However, this is not my primary concern. My biggest concern is that there are too many parents and their children – and nannies for that matter – who are leaving themselves wide open to prosecution or worse as a result of working outside the system.

I should add that this is not a problem unique to Australia – not by any means. Estimates are that as much as 85 per cent of in-home care in the US is provided by carers working outside the law. (It's hard to get a definitive figure locally, but something in the order of 65 per cent is probably about right.) There is also growing concern globally about the prevalence of modern slavery, with more and more stories coming to light of housekeepers, child carers and other home-based service providers working under horrendous conditions.

It is important that anyone who has any involvement in the childcare industry is aware of what is going on and what the risks are to those who choose to operate 'underground'.

And about time too

Of course illegal behaviour on the part of employers and employees is only of any consequence if the law is actually enforced. While the Australian tax laws governing contractors apply to any industry, until recently there has been little indication from the ATO that they had any interest in ensuring this was the case in practice for in-home child carers. In general it appears they've preferred to pursue more common contractor situations such as information technology and tradespeople. This 'blind eye' from the ATO was taken by many in our industry as tacit approval of their preferred way of operating, that is, of nannies working as contractors.

Finally, in 2016, we started hearing very strong noises from the ATO confirming what I've been arguing all along: that nannies cannot legally operate as independent contractors.

An ATO official investigating the tax implications of the Turnbull government's Nanny Pilot Programme confirmed that there are no circumstances – none – in which a nanny can be regarded as an independent contractor for tax purposes.

This applies to nannies working through government-approved and non-government-approved agencies as well as to nannies working privately. In none of these cases can a nanny be regarded as an independent contractor or as self-employed, regardless of whether or not they have an ABN. Rather, anyone working as a nanny must be an employee either of an agency or of the family they are working for.

This is a drum I've been beating for a long time. As I have pointed out very often to anyone prepared to listen, it has been quite clear for some time that nannies cannot pass the simplest tests required of independent contractors:

- Nannies typically have only one 'client'.
- Nannies cannot subcontract or delegate their work, i.e. they cannot pay someone else to do their work for them.
- Nannies are paid for the time they have worked, not a 'quoted price for an agreed or predetermined result'.
- Nannies do not take any commercial risks; their agency is legally responsible for the work they do.
- Nannies do not have full control over their work: agencies have the right to direct the way in which nannies do their work.
- Nannies do not operate independently of their agency. They work within and are considered part of the agency.

In other words, nannies cannot be regarded as running a legitimate business. They are employees, not contractors.

Why is this important? Because too many agencies and private employers have been getting away with underpaying their nannies by forcing them to act as contractors or, worse, paying them cash in hand.

This has short- and long-term consequences for both the nannies and our industry.

In the short term, aside from often being paid lower-than-award rates, nannies employed under these circumstances also miss out on superannuation payments and workers compensation. Often their working conditions are less than optimal as well, with long hours and their responsibilities spilling over into domestic chores.

The longer term consequences were well summarised in an article from American magazine *The Atlantic* (the situation in the US being arguably worse than it is in Australia).[1] As the article points out, both contract workers and those paid 'under the table' can quickly get left behind in the private economy:

> Without documented employment history, they lack access to better rental housing, improved terms for home and car loans, and opportunities to build a stronger credit history. In other words, it's like they've never held a job. Try getting a mortgage without any record of employment … These workers remain in the economic shadows, unable to build much of a financial future.

Of course we have recognised the prevalence of 'nannies as contractors' for a long time. The difference now is that the ATO, State Revenue Office Victoria and the Fair Work Commission seem to be turning their attention to our industry. Word is that they will look into nanny agencies, identifying instances of nannies and/or agencies that are operating outside the law. I suspect there will be quite a few concerned nanny agencies as a result of this.

Increased attention on the tax status of nannies, and of their

---

[1] www.theatlantic.com/business/archive/2014/03/the-immorality-of-evading-the-nanny-tax/359637/

wages and conditions as a result, comes at a time when wage fairness is prominent in the news. Recent underpayment scandals in large franchise chains such as 7-Eleven, Dominos and Grill'd are perhaps the most prominent examples, but there are numerous others coming to the surface. And those that appear in the media are only the tip of the iceberg.

An accountant I was speaking to recently told me that when he meets small business owners he always quizzes them on their understanding of employment law. He says it is quite clear that, despite the Fair Work laws having been in place for six years now, most employers remain ignorant of their legal obligations.

We have always believed that nannies deserve to be legally employed, properly respected and paid their full wage and entitlements. Thankfully my agency's clients have also shared this belief, and I am thankful that they believe in what we do. We are thrilled to be leading the way.

2

THE NANNYING INDUSTRY: HEADING IN THE RIGHT DIRECTION?

The more things change ...

I mentioned earlier that one of the passions I have outside of work is genealogy. Having grown up in Tasmania, there is always plenty of juicy convict history to delve into (not to mention finding a convict in the past of someone who thinks they have none). A few years ago I combined this interest with another – the Australians in World War I – when I visited the sites in Europe where my grandfather had fought with the 12th Battalion, one of the first to leave Australia after the start of the war.

The study of history always serves as a reminder of how much things change but also how much they stay the same. It's almost 30 years since I started Placement Solutions and looking back that same contradiction applies very much to the home-based childcare industry.

From my point of view, as someone inside the industry, what never changes is the satisfaction we get from dealing with both the kids and their parents. One of the great bonuses of home-based child care is that we, as carers, get to know our families really well – almost becoming part of the family at times. Because we see children in their home environment, we have the pleasure of seeing them change and grow up in myriad different ways.

The changes in the industry have, for the most part, been positive.

When I started offering a nanny placement service, in the late 1980s, what we now call nannies were seen as glorified babysitters. Most carers worked on an informal, casual basis and the pay was low, about $8 per hour. There were few, if any, standards applied to home-based child care. As a result of all this, being a nanny was not seen as something you did as a career. It was more of a fill-in job – something to do between 'real' jobs.

Over the years the professionalism of the home-based childcare industry has increased a lot, though it has continued to lag behind other areas of work. Bizarrely, the requirement for a Working with Children Check was applied to in-home child carers only after it became obligatory in almost every other industry involved with children. Even today, some people say the superannuation guarantee system does not apply to 'domestic workers', which includes nannies, though this is incorrect.

Given the central role that nannies play in children's lives, it has always seemed important to me that the industry be as professional as possible. That's why we invest significantly in ongoing training for our staff, apply strict standards to everything we do, and generally support any effort from governments to make the industry – including agencies, carers and clients – accountable.

There's still plenty of change to come. Much can be done in terms of professional development and peer support, particularly using the internet as a tool. No doubt the change will keep coming. In the end, though, the kids and families will always be the reason why we do what we do.

Increasing professionalism

One area in which there has been significant change over the last 30 years is the professionalism of the nanny industry, though on this count I have to say that our colleagues in the US have made more progress than we have in Australia. American nannies tend to have a very strong sense of themselves as a profession, which may be, at least in part, because of the sheer size of the industry. There are thousands and thousands of nannies in the US working in a whole range of situations. There are a lot of nannies who operate privately, and others who specialise in a particular area, such as Donna Robinson, the 'travelling nanny'. Donna's work is all related to travel, whether that means looking after children during a flight, helping them settle into hotels, or caring for them while their parents are busy elsewhere.

Another factor in the sense of professionalism found in US nannies is the high level of support they have from a range of prominent organisations. For a number of years I have been heavily involved with the INA, the International Nanny Association, which is based in the US and has as its members both nannies and nanny agencies. The INA provides scholarships for nannies and supports a Nanny of the Year award. I have made several friends within the organisation and we often chat about where the industry has been and where it is going.

Kellie Geres has been involved in the nanny industry for almost as long as I have. She was the INA's Nanny of the Year in 1997. Kellie took her first job as a nanny at the age of 19, moving from her home in northern Minnesota to New Jersey, not far from New York City. Her job interview at the time involved two phone calls and photos exchanged by mail. At that time, she says, 'everyone wanted a nanny from the Midwest'. She enjoyed the job from the start, especially watching her charges develop and playing a crucial role in helping them to 'be kids' with plenty of time spent outside.

Kellie worked for two families in Atlanta, Georgia, then moved to Pennsylvania and then to a family outside Washington, DC. She has been with that family since 1997, first as nanny to their two young children and, more recently, since those same children have moved away to college, as household manager.

It was in 1996 that Kellie's mother asked her, 'When are you going to get a real job? You can't be a nanny for the rest of your life'. The question caused a light-bulb moment for Kellie: she realised that being a nanny was a real job, and that it was a job she wanted to do for the rest of her life. Since then Kellie has been passionate about nannies seeing themselves as professionals – that is, in a *real* job – and she has pursued this passion via her membership of the INA. She eventually joined the INA Board and has played a leading role in helping the organisation to educate not only nannies, but also parents and the wider community in the importance of the nanny's role.

That education role is still important. In the internet era it has become much easier for parents to hire nannies directly, without the safety net of an agency's vetting of qualifications or background. '[The internet] can create a false sense of security', Kellie says. In the end, though, she believes the old adage that 'you get what you pay for' holds true, and professional nannies need to have the confidence to speak up if they are not being paid what they are worth or otherwise looked after properly.

Conferences like the annual INA Conference play an important role in not only educating nannies themselves but also in instilling a sense of professionalism. Two of our own nannies, Clare Carlisle Stranger and Cecily Laing, have attended INA conferences and witnessed this first hand. (Clare was the inaugural winner of the Placement Solutions Nanny of the Year in 2014 and Cecily won the same award in 2016. Both were nominated for the INA's international Nanny of the Year prize.) Clare and Cecily were struck by the energy and camaraderie that comes from around 200 nannies getting together in one place.

The formal sessions at these conferences play an obviously important role in the spreading and sharing of current knowledge; however, the opportunity to meet and share ideas is just as important. Clare commented after the 2014 conference that 'Nannying can be a lonely job and conferences like these are essential to overcoming this isolation'. All of us – in whatever capacity we hold in the industry – come away from such events knowing we are part of a global team of people dedicated to the welfare of children.

Other organisations and conferences play roles in supporting nannies and boosting professionalism through education and networking. National Nanny Training Day is an event organised by Sue Downey of Nannypalooza in which educational events are organised on a single day in cities all over the US and Canada. Nannypalooza (www.nannypalooza.com) hosts an annual weekend conference just for nannies which, as Donna Robinson puts it, 'makes many nannies feel connected and proud of what they do for the first time'. Nannypalooza also hosts a busy online forum for nannies all over the world.

The status of the nanny in the US has also been bolstered by the rise of firms offering specialist support to nannies, agencies and parents. Legally Nanny (www.legallynanny.com) is a law firm specialising in legal support for household and agency employers of nannies, and for businesses and individuals on home-based child care issues. The firm was founded by Bob King. HomeWork Solutions (www.homeworksolutions.com) provides tax and payroll services for household employers and agencies. And of course the Association of Premier Nanny Agencies (APNA) provides valuable support to the agency and placement sector of the industry.

In our own way we have been doing what we can to introduce some of the elements of US-style nanny professionalism to the Australian context. For years we have run regular professional development days for our nannies, bringing in guest speakers with something relevant to say for our industry. In 2016 we helped organise NannypaloozaOz, the first Nannypalooza conference to be held outside the US. Speakers at that conference included the organisation's founder, Sue Downey, and English nanny and advocate of nanny networking Helen McCarthy. Also in 2016 we took all this a step further with the establishment of Nurture Training College, a registered training organisation (RTO) offering formal training for nannies up to diploma level. It's the first college in Australia to offer such a specialist nanny focus.

For all of that, as I've said earlier and will say again, there is still plenty of improvement to be made. Despite advances and good support in many areas, recognition of nannying as a profession is far from universal in the US. In Australia, while the Australian Home Childcare Association (AHCA) provides valuable advocacy, we still lack a truly representative organisation for nannies, agencies and related businesses with the scope of the INA.

Wot's in a name,' she sez?

> Wot's in a name? -- she sez . . . An' then she sighs,
> An' clasps 'er little 'ands, an' rolls 'er eyes.
> 'A rose,' she sez, 'be any other name
> Would smell the same.'
>
> *C.J.Dennis, 'The Sentimental Bloke'*

Remember when 'human resources' was called 'personnel'? When 'team members' and 'associates' in department stores were called, simply, 'staff'? Over the years, the names of many jobs have been changed to improve perceptions of them. Sometimes these changes make sense, but sometimes they do nothing but cause unnecessary confusion.

A good example of the latter was a term that started to be used inside DEEWR (the former federal Department of Education, Employment and Workplace Relations, now the Department of Education) to refer to what you probably know as nannies and babysitters: 'early learning in-home childcare educators'. Thankfully that term seemed to disappear before it gained any traction (I wonder why!), though its appearance did serve to emphasise the fact that the child care industry is awash with misconceptions and ambiguities when it comes to 'who does what'.

Consider some of the names you will hear used within this industry today. *Au pair*, baby nurse, babysitter, nanny, doula, maternity nurse, mothercraft nurse, shadow mother, mother's help, new-born care specialist, night nanny, casual date night nanny, in-home child carer, maternity concierge. The list goes on. Considering that most parents have not had to deal with any of these terms before the birth of their first child, it's no wonder there is confusion and a blurring of lines across roles.

The INA has adopted a range of definitions for the various in-home care roles (you can read them at nanny.org/resources/families/in-home-child-care-definitions) but for the purposes of this book, I'd like to share some of the definitions we use within our own work.

- *Nanny*: a proactive carer who provides personalised care to children in their own home. Nannies can be casual, temporary or permanent, part time or full time, live-in or live-out. However, they are professionals at what they do, ideally qualified to (in the Australian context) Certificate III or Diploma level. They will also have a current first-aid qualification including an annual CPR refresh, and of course current police checks and or working-with-children checks relevant to the jurisdiction in which they work. In our agency, all nannies must have three years' verifiable childcare experience and demonstrable expertise.
- *Au pair*: a helper, usually without qualification or prior experience, who works typically for 15 to 30 hours per week acting in more of a 'big sister' role. An *au pair* should not be in

sole charge of children under school age. They do housework associated with the children but not general household chores, and they may do occasional evening babysitting or 'date night' care. *Au pairs* are great for live-in help before and after school for school-aged children. While not requiring a qualification, *au pairs* must have had first-aid training and a police check and attend an induction and debrief from their agency. *Au pairs* are generally paid an hourly wage from which board and rent are deducted with their informed consent. They should be provided with a furnished bedroom at a minimum.

- ***Babysitter***: in agency circles this is now a colloquial term that is not used professionally anymore. We would use the term 'casual date-night nanny' to separate professional nannies working on a casual basis from any informal 'babysitter' arrangement between families or neighbours.
- ***Child carer***: see nanny, though of course this term can be applied in a broader context to qualified carers working in long-day care situations.
- ***New-born care specialist***: This is a modern term for those who care for infants in the first six months. New-born care specialists are professional nannies who have undertaken specific additional training in the area of new-born care. They will often work for families with twins or other multiple births, help babies get into a settled routine and generally help parents, particularly the mother, get some rest. They will help day or night, feeding babies, sterilising bottles and performing childcare-related household duties.
- ***Baby nurse, mothercraft nurse, maternity nurse***: these terms are disappearing from popular use. Focused on the care

of new-borns, the contemporary equivalent is 'new-born care specialist'.

- **Mother's help or shadow mother**: also largely obsolete terms. The idea of a mother's help emerged between the wars after the era of live-in nannies and governesses. Often it would be a teenage girl who would do anything from peel the potatoes to play with the baby while its mother prepared a meal. The term 'parents' helper' is still used at times in the USA, but less so in Australia. 'Less than a nanny, more than a maid,' was the way these roles used to be seen.
- **Doula, midwife**: a midwife delivers babies and may also play a role in prenatal training of parents and postnatal check-ups. A doula's role is specifically to help the mother before, during and after birth. Neither doulas nor midwives are new-born care specialists unless they have also had the appropriate training.
- **Maternity concierge**: an 'estate manager' for the wealthy during and after pregnancy. Popularised by the television reality television show *Pregnant in Heels*.

I suspect the battle for clarity in the everyday use of these terms will never end. However, I do hope the day comes when at least those providing these various services – especially agencies – can be clear about the terminology they use so as to avoid adding to parents' confusion.

The importance of ethical and moral leadership

If we look back into history, we can find amazing stories of nannies who have worked through extraordinary circumstances.

One of the most memorable examples I have learnt about is the incredible role that a number of nannies took on in Europe during World War II. Since the war, 66 nannies have been recognised by the Jewish community as 'Righteous among the nations', or 'Righteous gentiles'. This honour is bestowed upon non-Jews who put their lives at risk to protect Jews during the holocaust.

It is believed that one of these nannies subsequently came to Melbourne, though so far I have not been able to track her down.

Guus Kaminsky was in her late teens when war broke out. Her parents headed an underground group in Holland that is reputed to have saved at least 37 lives. Guus herself helped one pregnant Jewish lady access medical attention, then arranged for the newborn child to be cared for by a local non-Jewish couple until the danger had passed.

Guus would regularly walk the baby in a pram to see his real parents. For another child, who was hiding with an aunt and uncle, Guus arranged for regular contact between the child and his parents, who were hiding elsewhere.

In the last few years another nanny has earned the right to be added to the list of Righteous gentiles. Sandra Samuel is an Indian nanny, a Christian, who was living at Jewish-run Mumbai Chabad House and working for the directors of the house, Rabbi Gavriel Holtzberg and his wife, Rivka. Sandra's main job was as nanny of the Holtzbergs' son, Moshe. When the house was raided during the 2008 Mumbai terrorist attacks, Sandra initially hid in a cupboard; but when she heard Moshe crying, she emerged and rescued the child – even though the attackers were still inside. He was left an orphan and subsequently Sandra moved to Israel with him so that he could grow up with members of his family.

The stories of Guus and Sandra are obviously extreme examples, but they deserve to be known because of each nanny's absolute commitment to the protective aspects of their role. In both cases they were willing to put their own lives at enormous risk in order to protect the children under their care. The stories serve to remind us of the selflessness that should be at the core of everyone in this industry, whether they are a nanny, running an agency or providing a related service.

• • •

For five years I had the opportunity to chair the Ethics Committee of the INA. Sounds a bit grand, doesn't it? 'Ethics' tends to come across as philosophical – as something we think and talk about rather than do. But nothing could be further from the truth.

Ethics is, in practice, no more than doing the right thing by others.

Taken a step further, it means doing the right thing not because you are being told to – through regulation or rule of law – but because ... well ... because it's the right thing to do.

Moral leadership is, to my mind, a close partner of ethics in that it carries with it the weight of expectation. To show moral leadership is to both demonstrate a highly ethical approach and in so doing to expect the same from others.

What does this mean with respect to nannies?

Ironically, given the expression 'nanny state', there aren't a lot of laws governing the behaviour of either nannies or nanny placement agencies. There are statutory requirements around things like Working with Children Checks and the provision of a safe working environment, but for the most part parents rely on nannies and their agencies to approach their work within a sound ethical framework.

In an effort to codify some general principles of expected behaviour, the INA developed a set of recommended practices for nannies and for nanny placement agencies. We do the same thing on a local level within my agency, via our Client Policy and Procedures Manuals, which have guidelines for our clients, carers and agency staff. Some of the INA-recommended practices for agencies are:

- Accurately and truthfully describe job duties and responsibilities, working conditions, hours, salary and benefits for in-home childcare opportunities.
- Help the nanny develop a written work agreement that accurately describes the conditions of employment arranged with the family.
- Make family information available to nanny candidates.

For nannies, the recommended practices include:

- Act as an advocate for young children.
- Respect each child as a unique individual.
- Create and maintain a safe and healthy environment for children.

Our agency code of conduct covers areas such as communication and confidentiality.

If all of this seems a bit obvious, or at least common sense, then that is probably a good thing. Overall, the aim of recommended practices and codes of conduct – of ethics in general – is to capture no more than what society as a whole would expect when it comes to the treatment of an employee (a nanny) by their employer (an agency), or of a carer (nanny) and the children she cares for.

That's not to say that those of us involved in this industry – parent, nanny or agency – don't benefit from reminding ourselves of these things from time to time, which is the point of having them written down. And while such codes are not legally enforceable, they do provide a basis for agencies like ours, or the INA, to be quite clear about the behaviours we expect of those who work under our names.

We also need to show moral leadership, by not only committing to codes of practice, but through our actions demonstrating that we actually believe in the premise of 'child first'.

Unfortunately this is not always the case. It is not uncommon to hear stories of 'small' compromises that indicate a failure of this leadership. The agency that says they thoroughly check all references but then fail to do so, or that is willing to employ a nanny without a face-to-face interview. The nanny who spends more time gossiping or complaining about her employers than she does focusing her attention on her charges. Both agencies and nannies who turn a blind eye to parental irresponsibility.

Some might say these things are quite minor in the overall scheme of things, but that is simply not the case. It's simply not ethical to say that you 'do the right thing'. It's not even enough to just 'do the right thing'. When we are prepared to compromise on basic standards, what sort of message does that send to the wider community about the importance of the work we do?

Every single person in our industry needs to be absolutely committed to the base principle that no child gets hurt on our watch. That means no corner cutting during recruitment and no getting distracted while on the job. It means holding others to account. Always.

We are lucky enough, at least in most Western countries today, that none of us will be asked to take the sorts of risk that Guus and Sandra took. We should show our gratitude for that by upholding our absolute dedication to the principle of 'child first' without compromise.

Remembering the 'care' in child care

Recently one of our nannies was providing regular respite care to the mother of a six-year-old child whose brother had significant special needs, as part of the service we offer to 'families in crisis'.

At one point the young boy turned to the nanny and asked, 'What do you do for a job?'

'I look after you', the nanny replied.

The boy paused and then said, 'I know you look after me, but what do you do for a job?'

'I'm your nanny. My job is to look after you.'

At that the child's little eyes filled with tears and he said, 'You mean you get paid to look after me?'

Until that moment the boy had obviously never considered the idea that someone could be paid to provide him with care.

Thinking quickly, the nanny replied, 'Yes, I do get paid, and I love my job. And I don't get paid any extra for loving you ... which I do'.

The reason I share this story is that it demonstrates so clearly the balancing act performed by government and service providers in the childcare sector, particularly when it comes to assisting vulnerable families.

On one hand the goal is simply to provide compassionate care: to give a vulnerable mother a break, to give a six-year-old boy something 'solid' to rely on (in this case a nanny), and to ensure the family gets back on its feet. In the medium term, 'crisis' care reduces the chance that the family will require ongoing government assistance beyond the norm.

On the other hand there is, as the young boy discovered, always a financial transaction involved in these situations. Where government subsidies are involved, there is a cost to the taxpayer.

To work, the balancing act requires special-needs cases to be properly assessed, service providers to work legally and efficiently, and government compliance to be followed to the letter.

My concern is that in recent years the balance is tipping towards a greater financial focus, with a detrimental effect on the child focus.

In effect, all providers and, more importantly, the children and parents who benefit, are being penalised. Or, looking at it another way, children in need are being penalised for something over which they have no control whatsoever.

We find a similar situation where a focus on 'work and study', ostensibly to encourage mothers back into the workforce as taxpayers, is being favoured for funding over simply providing care where it is needed. Again, the balance is tipping towards financial focus over a focus on care.

There needs to be a better way. A more compassionate, child-focused approach would be to ask, 'How do we get parents back to work or study while maintaining the necessary level of care to those children who need it?' A child-focused approach would be to see real value in child care as an end in itself, without it having to provide a financial return. A child-focused approach would be to recognise that in a healthy society sometimes we need to give the more vulnerable a helping hand.

Wouldn't it be wonderful if we all had the courage of my nanny, and were willing to say to the most vulnerable, 'We'll look after you', and that that was all that needed saying?

3
TRENDS IN CHILD CARE

There have been endless shifts in 'correct' or 'preferred' child care over the last 30 years, and the advent of the internet only seems to have caused those shifts to become more frequent. I have witnessed this not only in my professional work but also more recently as a new grandmother, having the opportunity to compare my approach with my daughter and her approach with her son.

Watching trends come and go over a number of decades does give you the opportunity to see past the nonsense, and believe me, there is no shortage of nonsense when it comes to advice on looking after our children.

In my work I've had the pleasure to get to know a number of experts doing really good work in parenting and child care – people who really know their stuff and are not interested in following trends for trends' sake. Rather they focus on the fundamentals, the aspects of child care that have never changed and likely never will. These people are always refreshing to talk to or hear, and I would suggest their advice is always worth listening to.

Getting back to 'good enough' parenting

One of the unfortunate ongoing trends of the last two or three decades, something exacerbated by the arrival of the World Wide Web, is a heightened fear of failure among many new parents.

This is a point made often by my friend, lactation consultant and author Pinky McKay. Pinky likes to compare the time when she had her own first baby in the 1970s with when she had her last in the 1990s. She points out that in the '70s parents had to trust their instincts because information was sparse. The upside was that there was not very much to fear. In contrast, since the mid-'90s and the advent of the internet, there is endless information and advice available. However, parents now have much greater expectations of themselves, and often perceive high expectations from others. They commonly experience a heightened fear of failure and they are much less inclined to operate instinctively.

Pinky is wary of anything that goes against a parent's instincts or a baby's natural rhythms – particularly any concept of rigid sleep patterns in the style of early 'guru' Truby King. She similarly disagrees with the idea of controlled crying – again because it works against both nature and parents' intuition. Crying, she reminded us, is the only way a baby has of communicating what it wants.

At one presentation Pinky gave our nannies she talked about the concept of 'the wonder weeks'. It comes from a book of that name by Dutch researchers Hetty van de Rijt and Frans Plooij. The 'wonder weeks' are critical periods of a baby's development when their perception of the world they are in makes a steep change. These weeks can produce changes in, for instance, sleep patterns that can then cause some parents to become worried that something is wrong. The truth is that some weeks will be better than others – just as they are for all of us when you think about it.

I think it's time there was a move back towards what I call 'good enough' parenting. Parenting has become excessively child centred, to the point of being unhealthy. Of course this doesn't mean parents should be neglecting their children, but rather there should be more of a balance. For kids to grow up healthy and resilient, they need their parents to also be healthy and happy. It's a bit like the way they tell us we should use the oxygen masks on an aeroplane: look after yourself first, then you'll be in a good position to help others. Put another way, the basic needs of a parent are just as important as those of a child.

Pinky encourages parents to disregard pretty much anything that they believe is 'expected' of them (or that they expect of themselves). Rather than making decisions based on maintaining control or meeting expectations, she would prefer parents applied three simple questions to any response they are considering: 'Is it safe? Is it respectful? Does it feel right?' When you think about it, those questions are relevant well beyond a child's infancy.

Most parents, if they look back to their own childhood, grew up with a lot more freedom than they give their children. I know I did. The parenting we all got was 'good enough' – and most of us turned out just fine. Perhaps it's time for modern parents to loosen the ties a little.

Loosen up and build resilience

I met Pittsburgh-based doctor Deborah Gilboa at an INA conference a few years ago. 'Dr G' has been a family doctor for over 15 years. She is the mother of four sons and appears regularly in the American media on the topic of parenting. She's also the author of *Get the behavior you want ... without being the parent you hate!*

Like the other advice I've been discussing, Deborah's advice is down to earth and timeless. It's built around three Rs that she believes every parent would like to see in their children: respect, responsibility and resilience.

> I want kids to express themselves respectfully (to know what that means and choose to do it most of the time), have a good work ethic, and handle it when things don't go their way. With these three Rs they'll be able to accomplish almost any goal they set for themselves.

In Deborah's view, too much parenting advice is premised on a particular philosophy of parenting, whether that be 'authoritarian' or 'attachment' or 'evangelical' parenting. She doesn't believe this is helpful – in practice every parent will be all of these things at different times. It's more useful to focus on those things – like respect, responsibility and resilience – that are essentially common goals.

Parents who can accept this are able to be more relaxed and flexible in their approach to parenting – to be closer to the 'good enough' parents I wrote about earlier. Importantly, they have the freedom to draw on the ideas and experiences of a great many others, regardless of background, culture or philosophy.

Of Deborah's three Rs, the one she is seeing many modern parents particularly grapple with is resilience. It's so easy to do things for our kids these days, but that doesn't mean that we should.

A great example of what this means in practice is our approach to entertainment. Somewhere along the way it seems to have become compulsory for adults to fill every available minute of their child's day. When a primary-school-aged child is attending three different after-school classes on a single day (yes, it does happen!) things are getting out of control. This sort of wall-to-wall diary leaves almost no time for parents to look after themselves.

Childhood expert Lisa Murphy, whose business is called Ooey Gooey, says something that I think is spot on: 'It's okay for children to be bored!' In other words, parents do not need to be the repositories of all entertainment; kids are more than capable of entertaining themselves if given the chance to do so. In fact, kids who are given the chance to be bored are far more likely to end up self-reliant than those who have every moment of every day planned for them. Deborah Gilboa agrees, pointing out that both responsibility and resilience are strengthened by children having ample unstructured time.

Another advocate of unstructured time is Louise Dorrat, an early childhood consultant and educator who spoke at one of our professional development days. She counsels less 'helicopter parenting' and more staying in the background when it comes to children's play. That means having the kids spend more time outside and just being left alone to play. It also means not constantly asking them what they're doing and just letting them get on with it. And it means not feeling like they need something new to do. Like Lisa Murphy, Louise likes children to be given the 'luxury' of getting to the point where they're bored. When it comes to play, your job is to be remain in the background.

From Louise's standpoint, kids need to be given more scope to be themselves than is often now the case. They don't need constant organised stimulation, and parents and carers should worry less about whether they 'are learning something today'. Louise speaks in terms of the three tenets of the Early Years Learning Framework (EYLF): belonging, being and becoming. Kids need to know where and with whom they belong. They need to have the chance to just be in the here and now. And we (carers and parents) need to recognise the importance of letting children become their individual resilient selves as they learn and grow.

The power of learning a musical instrument

With so many extracurricular activities on offer these days and, as I've said, the tendency to overschedule children's 'spare' time, it seems sensible that at least some of those activities have the potential to provide advantages in the long term. Learning a musical instrument, it seems to me, is a perfect example.

Lorenzo Capitanio runs the Music Education Academy in Melbourne's north-west and talks with some passion about the benefits music can give a child, not only in their childhood but throughout their lives. Lorenzo points out that there is strong research supporting the idea that children who learn a musical instrument often outperform their non-instrument-playing classmates in a number of academic areas, but particularly maths. Learning an instrument also teaches widely beneficial skills including patience, goal setting and perseverance.

Music has the benefit of offering both structure and unstructured opportunities to kids. Structure is necessary for a child (or adult) to master a musical instrument. Music lessons need to be regular, at least weekly, and they need to be supported by consistent practice. Lorenzo recommends a good routine of daily practice. It could be in the morning before school, straight after school, before or after dinner. Particularly in the early years, this will require commitment from parents too, as they encourage the formation of good practising habits and assist with practice.

However, the rewards of all this are many. Aside from boosting academic performance, playing music can build social skills and give children an outlet to explore their creativity. It can be a catalyst for meaningful unstructured play as they start to teach themselves new songs or even write their own. As their skills grow, musicians can take part in groups and ensembles like orchestras, in which they learn incredibly valuable teamwork and cooperation skills.

While there is undoubtedly educational and social value in some of the many activities children get involved in after school today, I suspect that reducing the number of pursuits in order to focus on a smaller number of activities with proven long-term benefits is a good way to find a balance and avoid overscheduling.

A simple truth: they want time with you

A year or so ago I found myself unexpectedly locked out of my daughter's house with my baby grandson. What to do? The answer was simple, but something many of us struggle with the concept of: nothing. It was no big deal. We just sat on the couch on the front verandah for an hour while we waited for my daughter to come back. The best part of the situation was that I did not have my mobile phone with me so the whole time spent with Reuben was 'hands free'. We just spent the time looking at each other, laughing and having fun.

It reminded me of an article I'd read some time back entitled 'What a "Hands Free" summer looks like' by Rachel Macy Stafford[2]. The article was written from a Northern Hemisphere perspective, but its relevance is universal in the age of the ubiquitous 'device'.

The gist of Rachel's article is encouragement to parents to lighten up a bit and be more present with their children. In particular, she

---

2 www.handsfreemama.com/2012/05/16/what-a-hands-free-summer-looks-like/

challenges parents to put away their mobile phones and other devices of distraction and spend time with the kids doing the simple things together.

Rachel refers to another article,[3] by teacher Erin Kurt, who over 16 years asked her students around Mother's Day what they remembered and loved most about their mothers. Over time she noticed similar responses being repeated and she compiled a 'top 10' list. The list is notable for its simplicity. There is nothing from these kids about buying gifts or taking them to lots of different activities. Rather, what kids really value is one-on-one time, basic togetherness, time to 'just talk' and being 'in the moment' with their parents.

The overall message here is something I think is well worth pausing to think about. When you have the chance to put your phone down for a while, will you do so? Is responding to that next Facebook notification really so important that it should disrupt real time with your child? When you look back at weekends and family holidays in years to come, what will stand out? The adventures you all got up to or the cat videos you watched?

At another of our professional development days we were entertained by performance storyteller Graham Davey. Graham's message was around reading and its importance to your children. He emphasised the role of belonging in home reading, arguing that kids see reading time as less about the book and much more about the opportunity to be with you. In fact he recommended that when reading to a child, you should choose the book – one that you enjoy reading – as this will make for a better experience for both of you. For the same reason, Graham also suggested that reading time should sometimes happen when kids are wide awake, not just before bed. (As an aside, I

---

3 www.lifehack.org/articles/lifestyle/the-top-10-things-children-really-want-their-parents-to-do-with-them.html

loved Graham's suggestion that you give your child a library card as an impromptu gift, something that they can use to access all the books they could ever want.)

In this era of online 'friends' it can be easy to undervalue genuine, fully present time spent together. Let's not forget that today's children arrive, like the children of any other era, with an innate need to form human relationships, especially with their parents.

The role of the modern grandparent

Before the birth of my first grandchild I, like most expectant grandparents, looked forward to being able to dote on him or her without having to take on the onerous responsibilities and sleeplessness of parenthood. I did feel well prepared, too. After all, I've been working with children in one way or another for my whole career. So I was a bit taken aback when my daughter, the mother-to-be, asked me whether I would attend a 'preparation for grandparenting' class with her.

'Don't you know what I do?' was my first response to her question, thinking that all my years in the childcare industry would be qualification enough. However, she continued to press and I eventually agreed to go.

It turns out I was wrong. Within about five seconds of the class starting, I realised that I knew almost nothing about being a grandparent in the 21st century.

It seems the most important 'job' of modern grandparents is keeping our mouths shut. Today's parents do their own research and they will ask for help if they need it. Until that point, the best thing we can do is provide them with meals.

How times have changed. After my first child neither my parents nor my in-laws offered much advice at all – they claimed to have forgotten all the important stuff. I was left largely to navigate on my own but without, of course, the guidance of Google.

When I had my second child eight years later, the grandparents' memories had magically been revived.

I remember my father – a country bank manager – offering advice on breastfeeding. I should ignore, he said, the rigid feeding regimen of Truby King and the Plunket Society, whose advice my mother had followed with me. Salient advice from an unlikely quarter.

My mother-in-law, a successful businesswoman and orchestral violinist, chimed in with her views, while my mother's 'practical' assistance included cutting the feet out of my baby's grow suits. (She was worried that they would lead to disfigured feet akin to ancient Chinese foot binding.)

The gist of today's advice seems to be that grandparents should no longer need to tread on eggshells around their offspring and *their* offspring. We should be able to relax into our new role, confident that if our help is needed it will be asked for. Time will tell whether it works out that way in practice.

I think it will depend a lot on the parents, and here I can see parallels with nannies. Some of our clients look to their nannies as teachers – as people who can share their expertise about child care – while other clients hold strong opinions of their own and prefer a nanny to essentially be 'seen but not heard'. There is no 'one size fits all' here.

When my father wasn't giving breastfeeding advice he was fond of a saying often attributed to Mark Twain, along the lines of: 'When I was seventeen, my father was so ignorant I could hardly stand to have the old man around. But when I got to twenty-one, I was astonished by how much he'd learned.' Perhaps if I manage to keep my opinions to myself, my daughter and her husband might eventually realise that I've learned a bit along the way too!

From the distance of a couple more years, now being 'granny nanny' to a toddler, I can safely say everything I learned at grandparenting class was completely true and I have passed this advice on to friends as they enter the world of grandparenthood.

It's not all black and white: welcome progress in perinatal depression

One of the most welcome developments in child care in the last 20 years or so has been the increasing awareness of, and willingness to talk about, postnatal and antenatal depression. For far too long the 'baby blues', as they were quaintly referred to in the 1950s and '60s, were waved away as just one of those hormonal issues that some mothers had to deal with.

However, the work of organisations like PANDA (Perinatal Anxiety and Depression Australia) is far from complete.

My agency has been a sponsor of PANDA for a couple of years now. For over 30 years, PANDA have been providing support to mothers and fathers who suffer from mental health problems associated with pregnancy and the period after child birth (collectively known as the perinatal period). The Melbourne-based organisation runs a national helpline staffed by PANDA employees and volunteers. It is the only Australian helpline dedicated to this condition and it takes around 11,000 calls per year. In addition, PANDA works to provide community and professional education and a range of other support activities, including playgroup facilitation and support referrals.

The statistics for perinatal depression and anxiety may surprise you. In Australia around 100,000 expecting and new parents suffer the symptoms every year – that's nearly 2000 per week. Perhaps more surprising is that around a quarter of that number are fathers: up to one in 20 men are affected pre- and/or post-pregnancy. What this statistic makes clear is that perinatal mental health issues are not just biological or hormone related. In both men and women there can also be underlying psychological and social issues.

If left untreated, the effects of these issues can be dreadful, including threatening the relationship between parents and damaging the precious early relationship with a newborn baby.

The good news is that there is support available and, particularly with early intervention, these conditions can be managed and mitigated.

The bad news is that, despite increased awareness, too many expecting and new parents still put up with antenatal and postnatal depression and anxiety without seeking help. Whether it is fear of the stigma of 'failed parent', thinking that they are alone in their suffering, or simply lack of awareness that help is available, far too many people try to struggle through these issues on their own.

PANDA is working to build community awareness – not only among expecting and new parents, but also in the wider community. Very often partners, friends, colleagues, relatives – and nannies – are in a better position to identify the symptoms than the sufferers themselves. PANDA's main message is that *It is okay to talk about it*, and doing so early on could save a lot of unnecessary suffering.

PANDA encourages everyone in the community to take time out

and learn the symptoms of antenatal and postnatal depression and anxiety. Their websites – www.panda.org.au and www.howisdadgoing.org.au – both provide information and strategies that everyone can use to potentially help someone who is suffering, or at risk of suffering, from these conditions.

I'm very proud of our sponsorship of PANDA, as we share a common goal of supporting new parents and their families.

4

THE ROLE OF TODAY'S NANNY

When he was New York's mayor, Michael Bloomberg introduced a range of laws in his city aimed at improving the health of its people. One of the most controversial of these laws was a proposed limit on the size of soft drink (soda) cups available at fast food outlets, cinemas and so on. His efforts were lampooned by a number of the local news outlets, with the *New York Post* running a cartoon of Bloomberg dressed as Mary Poppins. Bloomberg's response was that it was 'one of the most wonderful cartoons I've ever seen'. He went on, saying that being depicted as a nanny was 'a great badge of honour ... It says we're trying to do something — save lives'.

This story serves as a perfect example of the diverse community views of the role of the nanny. On one hand we have the age-old portrayal of the nanny as a disciplinarian – a perspective that pervades today in the frequent derogatory use of the term 'nanny state'. On the other hand we have recognition of the nanny as a dedicated carer, as someone who 'saves lives'. In between, nannies are often confused with *au pairs* and babysitters, and thought by some to be housemaids, cooks and cleaners.

My view is that a nanny is a professional carer of children, usually in their own home. She (in the vast majority of cases a nanny is a 'she') plays the role of educator, playmate, carer and, yes, occasionally, disciplinarian. The wellbeing of the children in her care is always her first priority.

However, it is never as straightforward as that.

The many faces of the nanny

The potential breadth of the nanny's role was well summarised by our 2016 Placement Solutions Nanny of the Year, Cecily Laing, when she described her career in her application for the award:

> I've been a live-in, live-out, full-time, part-time, temp, paid on the books, paid under the table nanny over the years. I've lived in multiple states (I even lived in remote Coober Pedy!). I've had sole charge, had stay-at-home mums, had work-at-home dads, had maternity-leave mums, had newborns to 10-year-olds, worked with able-bodied kids and physically disabled kids. I've worked for many different cultures, travelled with families domestically and internationally, travelled with only the children, taken kids on holidays without their parents and been on family holidays. I've stayed overnight, been a day nanny, joined mothers' groups, play groups, done kinder duty, volunteered in the school classroom, organised activities, organised events, run households and worked with other staff. I've had long-term positions and short-term positions. The list goes on!

One thing Cecily doesn't mention is the role of diplomat.

A few years ago I put one of our nannies forward for a position in London. She had an interview with the client that seemed to go well. At the end of the interview the client's husband walked in and the client turned to the nanny and asked, 'Don't you think my husband's handsome?'

The nanny looked the husband up and down and said, 'I suppose he's alright'.

The next thing she knew, she was being chased down the road, having forks thrown at her. We still don't know what would have happened if she had provided a different answer. Perhaps it would have been the husband chasing her down the road? However, this nanny did learn one thing, and that is that one of the roles of a professional nanny is as a diplomat. A nanny has no opinion about the handsomeness of someone's husband. Her only answer can be, 'I have no opinion on this matter. I'm a professional nanny'.

Another time a woman rang me and explained what she was looking for by way of a nanny. It all sounded straightforward, though I was a little concerned that she stated that the nanny must be 'dressed appropriately' because her child went to a private school and she wouldn't have the nanny turning up in thongs or leggings and so on. Nevertheless, I took that on board, knowing that our nannies would meet that requirement in any case. Then, just before we were going to end the call, she said, 'Oh, and most important of all, I won't have a good-looking nanny'. Now it was my turn to be diplomatic, explaining that we don't grade our nannies on their looks. Her reply was that her previous husband had left with the last nanny, and she now had a new baby with a new husband and was not going to lose this one. She insisted that she would not have a good-looking nanny. The bottom line on this request seemed to be that a nanny must be smart but not attractive. Whatever that means. My thought was that perhaps she should have been more careful in choosing her husband.

Unfortunately one of the requests we get more often than we should is for nannies who will be able to help with domestic tasks. We had an enquiry from a lawyer who said her nanny had quit and would be hard to replace because not only had she been great with the kids, but the year before she had whipped up a dress for this lady for Melbourne Cup Day, and she had also made tins and tins of Christmas shortbread that the lawyer had distributed as her own handmade work gifts. As in all these cases, my staff and I will explain, tactfully, that a professional nanny is a child carer and not a domestic assistant. If a household manager is what the client is after, we can help them with that, but it will be a different person.

While most nannies work with their charges in the children's home, that's not always the case. Donna Robinson is one exception. Donna spends some of her time as a specialist nanny for newborns, but she also has clients who travel, and with whom she travels. For one of her clients, she literally travels halfway around the world and back – between Perth and Boston – twice a year. It's not hard to see how she came to call herself 'the travelling nanny'! Donna happened to start her nannying career around the time that the internet was gaining widespread use. This helped her to find temporary nannying opportunities, often working with the parents of newborns who had found themselves in difficulty for one reason or another. Over time she started travelling with families on vacation, allowing the parents to have some couple time, and this has become a major part of the work she does, along with continuing to care for newborns.

Of course, at a more basic level, many nannies play an important role in helping to 'level out' the workforce. In her popular book, *Lean In: Women, work and the will to lead*, Facebook COO Sheryl Sandberg lists a number of barriers to women's progress. 'Too few workplaces offer the flexibility and access to childcare and parental leave that are necessary for pursuing a career while raising children', while '[women] continue to do the majority of the housework and childcare'. None of this will be surprising to any woman trying to balance a career with motherhood, and it is remarkable to me, more than 20 years since I had my daughters, that very little has changed in these areas. For many women trying to match it with men in senior management roles, a nanny plays a critical enabling role.

One of my long-term clients was a Melbourne woman who came to us not long after she was appointed to head up her organisation. She came in to see me when she was very pregnant, with a huge red neon trouser suit over her large belly, and asked me what she had to do to get a great nanny and then keep her. I told her she needed to pay her properly and look after her. I sent her a Scottish nanny called Margaret. I also suggested to her that she ask her board of directors whether they would fund a housekeeper and a nanny for her, which they agreed to do. This client kept that nanny for 17 years. At one stage people started making jokes about why she had had a nanny for so long, though in truth she was a single mother who, running a prominent organisation, was often asked to travel overseas and at those times her school-age son needed a carer. I have no doubt that Margaret played an important role in enabling this woman to remain in her leadership role for nearly two decades.

Aside from these examples are the nannies who do surprising things outside their work. One of the most prominent of these has to be Vivian Maier. Vivian worked as a nanny in Chicago from the mid-1950s until the later '90s. She was a very private person, keeping entirely to herself outside of her work. As a result of this guardedness, no one was aware that in her leisure time Vivian was a photographer. She walked the streets of Chicago with a twin-lens Rolleiflex camera, capturing candid images and portraits of ordinary people. It wasn't until shortly after she died, in 2007, that the extent of her photographic record would come to light. Over 100,000 negatives were discovered, by chance, at a 'thrift auction'. Among these images is some of the most vivid and striking urban photography of the 20th century. Within a year this otherwise ordinary nanny came to be recognised as one of the most important photographers of her generation. Her photographs of poor children are particularly strong, perhaps reflecting the sensitivity of her profession.

Putting the child first

Of course the most important role of the nanny is child carer, though even here we need to be clear about definitions. The professional nanny is a child development specialist. Her job is not simply to watch over the children and make sure they don't come to any harm. It is to interact with her charges, often for many hours each week, during a period of their lives when they are developing very quickly. As Cecily Laing puts it, a nanny helps 'shape little people into awesome little humans'.

If we look back at the childcare trends I wrote about in the previous chapter, nannies can play an important role in helping parents to navigate the expectations they have brought to parenthood. As Pinky McKay puts it, nannies are in a wonderful position to 'gently show the way', providing reassurance and encouragement to new mums and dads.

Dr Deborah Gilboa points out that parents who are willing to be open minded in the way they interact with their nannies, willing to take advantage of their nanny's expertise and see their feedback for what it is and not as criticism, have a huge advantage. 'They have a child development specialist spending a large number of hours each week with their kids, in their own home.' The best scenario is where parents and their nanny are able to share a goal for a particular child, then work towards that goal cooperatively. This requires trust and communication, of course, but it also requires the nanny to be willing to see herself as a child development specialist.

Deborah shared the example of building resilience as a joint goal. Building resilience often means kids not automatically getting things their own way – and unfortunately when in-home child care is involved, it can be the nanny who bears the brunt of the push-back when this happens, so it is important that the task is treated as a team effort between nanny and parents. First it's essential to agree on a goal, and on a strategy to get there (e.g. no television until the playroom is tidied up). Then, should things get chaotic, try to meet the parent at the door and say something like, 'I'm happy to see you. Remember we agreed to work on Johnny tidying his room? Well, we've been working on that and what you're about to see and hear is Johnny's reaction to learning that responsibility.' She emphasises that in situations like this the parents also need to hold firm:

> It's really hard as a caregiver when you agree with the parents that the kids should have a couple of chores to do when they get home from school, and you're willing to take charge of them doing those things, but then you have the parents arriving home, greeted by a tantrum and opting just to quieten things down by placating the child – and undoing all your hard work in the process.

The same applies to things like unstructured play. Obviously this doesn't mean the nanny spending her time on Facebook while the children roam free but, again in concert with the parents, nannies should be able to feel comfortable giving children some unstructured play time at some point during the day. Similarly, nannies should be comfortable imposing rules about screen time (small or large).

Perhaps the most prominent role of the nanny, after child carer and 'child development officer', is that of communicator ... with her client parents. Maintaining open communication, both informally and formally (via, say, weekly meetings), is absolutely fundamental to a successful ongoing relationship between client and nanny.

Child protection

Sadly, child abuse in all its forms is still all too common in Australia and many other countries, and the community's attitude to child abuse is still surprisingly relaxed. A recent survey by Child Wise, a not-for-profit child sexual abuse prevention organisation, returned some remarkable statistics, including:

- Of adult respondents, 20 per cent did not identify the actions of a parent who hits their child on the head as child abuse.
- Only 30 per cent of adult respondents said they would believe a child who said they had been abused.
- Only 3 per cent of abused children will ever tell of their abuse.
- Only around 5 per cent of child sex offenders have been caught and convicted for their crimes.
- Emotional abuse is the most substantiated abuse type, followed by neglect and then physical abuse.

In many Australian states and territories, as in most of the US, nannies and all other child carers now have mandatory reporting responsibilities. In our state of Victoria this took too long, and in fact my agency took the issue into its own hands and implemented our own child protection policy ahead of the government's. We have also been accredited by Child Wise to run their 'Speak Up' short course, focusing on how to prevent, recognise and respond to instances of child abuse, and all our office staff and nannies have attended the program.

Continuing self-improvement

One of the characteristics of taking on the mantle of 'professional' is a commitment to continuing education and self-improvement. This has long been understood in professions such as medicine and law, where there is an obvious need to be 'up with the latest'. However, it is no less relevant to the nanny profession. Continuing development simply helps nannies do a better job, with more confidence and less stress (not to mention better pay).

As we have already discussed, childcare trends are coming and going all the time. Laws come and go too – mandatory reporting requirements being one example. As Sue Downey, the founder of Nannypalooza, puts it, 'to get better at what they do, and to stay fresh and motivated and avoid burning out, nannies need to take the initiative to stay up-to-date with new ideas'. Or as professional organiser Tanya Lewis told us on one occasion, nannies need to 'make sure they have the tools needed to do their job, and keep them sharp'.

Tanya was talking in part about equipment like toys, books and a resource folder, but her message applies equally to education and self-improvement.

Within my agency we've promoted continuing development through regular professional development days. More recently we launched a separate educational arm, Nurture Training College, Australia's first and only registered training college offering courses up to diploma level specifically designed for nannies by a veteran of the industry.

The college has enabled us to run regular specialist training too, such as the newborn care program developed by Tonya Sakowicz and the Child Wise 'Speak Up' program I mentioned earlier.

Then, as I noted in Chapter 2, there is networking, whether that be attending conferences, taking part in online forums or simply meeting up with a group of other nannies once in a while. Anything to break the isolation and refresh the energy and enthusiasm for the wonderful work nannies do.

The 10 habits of great nannies

So let's remind ourselves of those things that contribute to the making of a great nanny. Here's a list of the 10 things I think really good nannies tend to do constantly, in no particular order:

1. Put children first
Great nannies always make the interests of the children in their care their top priority. *Always*. For instance, if a nanny finds herself drawn to an external activity such as a regular morning tea with other nannies and their charges, she will first ask herself whether that gathering is providing real benefit to the children. Her own need for social interaction comes second.

2. Communicate with parents – formally and informally
Keeping the communication channels open is absolutely essential for an ongoing, successful relationship with your clients. This is best done both

formally, such as via a handover diary and regular review meetings, and informally with quick conversations at the start and end of the day.

3. Take on constructive criticism

As hard as it is to do, we all need to be aware of our weaknesses, and one of the best ways to do that is to be open to the constructive observations of those around us. Try not to take criticism personally: focus on the behaviour that could be changed, not on the feelings associated with having someone suggest that you're not perfect.

4. Be diplomatic

It can be difficult at times, particularly if a nanny finds herself the meat in the sandwich of a disagreement between parents, but unless it is a matter on which you can express a professional opinion, you're best to express no opinion at all.

5. Stay in tune with your own needs and those of the children

As children grow, their needs inevitably change. Sometimes that can lead to the need for some hard decisions. If you're most comfortable working with infants, for instance, then there might come a time, when your charge is about three years old, that you need to be willing to call time and move on to your next job.

6. Constant and continuous learning

Unless a nanny remains open to improvement, she will never be able to stay up to date and maintain the highest professional standards.

7. Networking

This is really an extension of continuous learning. It is so easy in our profession to fall into the trap of developing 'your way' of doing things and then becoming complacent. Similarly, it can be easy to put up with challenges without seeking help. Staying in touch with other nannies – both face to face and online – is the perfect way to avoid both of these.

8. Know your rights

I've written about this many times before, but to succeed as a great nanny in the long term you need to know and assert your legal rights. For example, do not accept domestic duties that go beyond those of a nanny, and do not accept work from an agency that requires you to operate as a contractor with your own ABN.

9. Know your obligations

This is the flip side of the previous point. As a professional nanny you need to be clear about your responsibilities, particularly with respect to duty of care over the children you are looking after and mandatory reporting requirements.

10. Only work with accredited agencies that operate within the law

Again, I've written about this often, but no matter how tempting it is to do otherwise, you should only ever work with an agency that will employ you legally, that has thorough selection, placement and monitoring processes, and that provides ongoing professional development opportunities.

5

THE ROLE OF THE PARENT

A nanny's success can never be achieved entirely on her own. Her role is necessarily as part of a team alongside her clients, typically the parents of the children she cares for, and our agency. Our best results have always come when the parents understand the nanny's role and play a proactive role in the selection of their nanny, in ongoing and regular communication with her, in providing her with the best possible working conditions and, ultimately, in managing the 'separation' when she moves on.

What to remember when hiring a nanny

Thirty years of running a nanny agency has taught me a thing or two about what works and what doesn't when it comes to choosing a nanny. Whether you are hiring your first nanny or your fourth, the same principles apply if you choose to do the hiring yourself.

Know why you are hiring a nanny

Start by being really clear about why you are hiring a nanny, and have a clear job description. A nanny is someone who will provide proactive, professional child care for your children in their own home. She is not a housekeeper, a personal assistant or a home renovator. She is not even a babysitter, in the sense of someone who passively minds the kids. It is amazing how often this is misunderstood. A clear job description is essential, right from the beginning, in order to avoid potential confusion and misunderstandings. (My agency can provide help with compiling this if you need it.)

Screen and reference check

Be careful to screen applicants properly, including reference checks. This is obviously really important, but as it can be time consuming there's a tendency to cut corners.

I once had a woman come to see me who was a qualified nanny who had just emigrated from England. That meant her referees were in England too, and I would have to call them in the very early hours of the morning my time. In this case there was a bonus, though. On her list of referees was a very familiar name: John Cleese, one of my comic heroes. I rose at three in the morning – passing my husband in the living room watching an Ashes test match from England. I made the call and on hearing the voice on the other end of the line I knew immediately that it was Cleese himself who had answered. I explained that I was calling to check a reference. 'Apparently you suggested that she come to Australia', to which he replied that he couldn't have thought much of her if he'd suggested she come to Australia. He then gave her an excellent reference. Towards the end of the call he asked me if that was the cricket he could hear in the background, and I explained that my husband was up watching it. He asked if my husband supported Australia, to which I replied, 'Of course'. Then Cleese said, 'Put him on'. I said to my husband, who looked at me in disbelief, 'John Cleese is on the phone and wants to talk to you'. Cleese went on to enthusiastically exchange cricketing tips and told my husband why Australia was going to win this match.

Not every early-morning reference call will be that entertaining, but they are all important.

Make sure that you are shown the originals – not copies – of documents like a current Working with Children Check and written references. It is always a good idea to check written references with a phone call as well. Obviously if you are using an agency they should be checking these documents for you, but there's nothing to stop you asking to see them as well. It's also wise to agree on a trial period to make sure that all the various parent/nanny/child relationships look like they are going to work. This benefits everyone involved.

Make a formal hiring agreement

Nannies must be formally employed – by the child's parents or an agency – and paid the award wage as a minimum. Nannies cannot be employed as contractors working under their own ABN, nor for cash payments. These are both illegal and could get both you and the nanny into hot water. In the case of contracting, this has been the case since 2010. This is because, as I've already explained, contractors, under the ATO definition, must be operating as if they were a business. That means setting their own working conditions, such as hours of work and job description, and replacing themselves with someone else if necessary. None of these apply to in-home child care.

Along the same lines, you will also need to make arrangements for regular superannuation payments into the nanny's fund, as well as organising workers compensation insurance and 'pay as you go' tax instalments. All this can get complicated and time consuming, which is why many people choose to use an agency with a full and separate payroll service. However, whether you employ and pay your nanny yourself or through an agency, the important thing to remember is that she is an employee and so entitled to the same rights as any other employee.

Create a development plan

Parents who want to keep their nanny in the long term will want to invest in her development. It pays to make plans from the outset to give your nanny professional development opportunities.

Being a nanny can be a lonely experience in many ways. As much as all nannies love working with their children, they need adult conversation as well. Most don't usually get to even speak to an adult except at the start and end of the day, and interaction with others in their profession can be very rare indeed. For this reason we put a lot of emphasis on creating frequent professional development opportunities for all our nannies. They give carers a great chance to bounce ideas off one another (while keeping details, including names, confidential), as well as keeping them in touch with all the latest thinking in child care and related areas. Professional development keeps nannies energised and excited about their work.

Choosing an agency

Deciding to use an agency for your nanny is a great way to bypass the challenges of having to source the right person and manage the administrative aspects of their employment. However, how do you choose an agency when they all sound great (that's called marketing!) and you don't know anything much about any of them? Obviously I'd love you to ring my agency, but of course it won't suit everyone. However, there are a number of things I strongly believe you should look for when considering a nanny agency.

First and most basically, you need to feel comfortable before you make your decision. You need to talk to the agency and be satisfied that they are a professional operation with systems in place at every level, from recruitment through to job monitoring and dealing with issues. A good test for this is whether, when you are face to face with someone at the agency, they are happy and comfortable with you asking as many questions as you need to ask in order to satisfy yourself of their bona fides.

Some of the questions you might like to ask are:

- What is their smoking policy? Many agencies will have a complete non-smoking policy. It is a condition of our contract with the federal government for the provision of funded child care that neither the nanny nor the parents smoke around the children. We extend this policy, at least as far as nannies are concerned, to non-funded placements as well.

- What professional development opportunities does the agency make available to their nannies? Do they actively promote the development of their nannies? Do they see value in education for their nannies?

- What does the agency understand and enact in the way of the rights and obligations of their nannies? Do they only accept (or even require) nannies working as independent contractors? If so, you might be cheeky and ask why, given the illegality of such an arrangement. Does the agency pay superannuation and organise workers compensation insurance?

- Does the agency have documented, current policies covering areas such as privacy, child protection and mandatory reporting, employment standards and so on? Can you read those policies?

- Do they have testimonials from clients? Can they put you in touch with some of their clients and nannies who would be willing to vouch for your service?

- What is their recruitment process? Do they meet all shortlisted nannies face to face as part of the selection process? Do they call referees or rely just on printed references?

- Under what circumstances, if any, does the agency decline to work for a client?

- What professional associations does the agency belong to, such as the Australian Home Care Association (AHCA) or International Nanny Association (INA) or Association of Premiere Nanny Agencies (APNA)?

- Does an agency representative conduct occasional but regular in-home visits to discuss progress with both the nanny and the clients? Will you be able to meet with someone at the agency's offices should the need arise?

That list might seem long, but you have to remind yourself that it is your children who are being discussed here. If, in the end, you discover that hiring a nanny through an agency that can answer these questions is prohibitively expensive, you may need to question whether an alternative form of child care might work better for you, such as long-day care. Yes, of course there are cheaper agencies out there, and you can even hire a nanny straight off a website, but is it really worth the risk? And are you happy with the fact that ultimately, if you are providing your nanny with below-award pay and conditions, you are stealing from the nanny, and ultimately from your own child?

The fact is that using a professional nanny will also be a more expensive option simply because the nanny is providing individual, personalised care to your child. They are providing a premium service, and such services always require an investment.

How to keep your great nanny

When you've found a great nanny it makes sense to want her to stay, at least until you reach a point when your children no longer need a nanny's care. As it turns out, provided your nanny is happy in the first place (which her job performance would indicate is the case), looking after a few basics should see her remaining with you for a while.

First and foremost, give her the respect she deserves as a professional and expert at her job. A nanny is not just a babysitter 'watching over' the children. Nor is she a 'little bit of help' for the family. A nanny is a parents' helper providing one-on-one care to your most precious assets while you're at work or meeting other commitments. Your nanny will provide your children with structure and education while keeping them happy, healthy and safe.

Remember that your home is your nanny's workplace, just as the office or school or retail store is the workplace of people who work outside of the home. As such, the work conditions you provide for your nanny should equate to what she would expect in any other workplace. The environment should be safe. She should be treated as a person, not a servant. She should not be expected to perform roles substantially beyond her job description.

A nanny should certainly not be expected to act as a housekeeper. Nannies do child-related housework, such as meal preparation, cleaning up after the child and so on, but no more than that. You wouldn't ask your accountant to wash the dishes at work, so the same should apply to your nanny. Aside from the disrespect inherent in such an expectation, never forget that your nanny's passion and energy need to be directed at helping your children to grow and learn. That's their job, and it shouldn't be diminished by routine chores.

Of course it should go without saying by this point that keeping your nanny happy also requires that you pay her legally and properly, and that you provide her with her entitlements – again just as she would expect in any other workplace.

And finally, like any relationship, a good nanny–client relationship depends on communication for its ongoing strength. So keep talking to her, checking in daily on progress and having regular reviews to make sure that any and all issues are on the table and being dealt with.

Managing live-in and long-term nannies

Live-in and long-term nannies are often a special case because inevitably, over the course of time, professional boundaries can become blurred, or risk doing so. There are a few 'rules' – perhaps we should call them guidelines – that are worth keeping in mind. Most of these apply to all nanny–client relationships but they are particularly relevant to the longer term nanny or the nanny who lives with you.

First and foremost, everyone needs to remember that the nanny is doing a paid job and therefore there need to be boundaries. For live-in nannies this means physical boundaries: her own space that is genuinely her own. Children need to understand that when the nanny is in her room, she's 'off duty' and should be left alone. Or perhaps the rule can be that when the door is shut she should be left alone, whereas when it is open the children may say hello. It depends on the nanny and the arrangement. The important thing is that some sort of signal exists.

These boundaries need to be maintained, particularly when the kids are around, as they won't be able to distinguish between 'work' and socialising. Sitting down with the nanny for a glass of wine after she has officially finished work on a Friday afternoon is not a good idea. Worse still is where these sessions are used to complain about your other half while they are not around. Remember that your nanny answers to both parents and that that relationship shouldn't be undermined by one parent or the other.

Boundaries need to be clear at the start of the day too. If you leave early for work, leaving the children in the nanny's care, it is not acceptable that the nanny stays in bed until the children wake her after you leave. A nanny needs to be up and ready for work as soon as she is required, which means before you leave.

The other thing to note about longer term nannies is that those factors that lead to success in any nanny–client relationship don't diminish in importance over time. Factors like showing respect to each other, having clear agreements about responsibilities, sharing routine handovers both verbally and in writing, and conducting regular performance reviews – these shouldn't drop off just because your nanny has been with you for a few years.

Jealousy and the nanny

You've found yourself a fantastic nanny. The kids love her, and you no longer need to worry about their care or feel guilty for being at work. Now everything should be rosy, shouldn't it? So why doesn't it feel that way? This is more common than you may think, and is something to be aware of.

Say the term 'jealousy of the nanny' out loud and you're likely to be greeted with sniggers as people imagine a story from *New Idea* in which a famous husband runs away with a nanny 20 years his junior.

While that can happen, it is very rare. Far more likely is that the mother of the house becomes jealous of the nanny for a host of other reasons. The nanny is getting to spend lengthy, quality time with the child or children. She is dedicated to the task of spending time with them, not having to juggle doing the dishes, thinking about dinner, arranging an electrician and planning the diary for next week. The nanny's focus is something most parents rarely get to enjoy.

Then there can be the situation where the child won't come willingly into your arms when you get home. This can be because they are tired, they've had a busy, fun day or, particularly with very young children, they are a bit confused. All of this is quite normal and no reflection on you as a parent, but there is no denying it can be hurtful at the time. And after all that, the nanny gets to clock off and go home, just as you've arrived home exhausted and now have to organise the evening routine.

Sometimes jealousy can emerge from a sense that the nanny will be loved by the child more than you will. In my view this is something that just needs to be dealt with – if your child is getting on with the nanny that well, then you have made a good choice. There is no doubt that your love as a parent will always be what your child wants, and gives, most and, frankly, the most mature approach will be to understand that, roll with it and accept that what you have done is add a new person of good character to your child's life.

A byproduct of nanny jealousy can be an unconscious desire to outdo the nanny. When my daughters were young we had a nanny with an Italian background and she would cook a lovely spaghetti Bolognese for the girls – so good that they often asked for more. My husband decided that he had to match this, so went about cooking his own version of the pasta dish, only to be miffed when it was not received with such alacrity.

An often unspoken source of jealousy can be the youth of the nanny, in those cases where the nanny is young (they aren't all so!). There she is, curled up on the floor with your child, enthusiastically playing with glitter as if she's on the set of *Play School*. If you tried to do that all you'd be thinking about is the pins and needles you're going to get in your feet and the cleaning up that's going to be needed afterwards. And yes, that youth can attract the attention of a husband but, as I said, situations where that goes any further than a furtive glance are less common than you probably think (and, in truth, probably indicative of deeper problems in other areas).

To my mind the way to look at any of this is to accept it for what it is and get on with things. In truth, if your nanny getting on well with your child is the worst situation you have to deal with then you are very lucky, and your child is even luckier. Your nanny could be more hands off, frequently distracted by Facebook and always talking to her boyfriend on the phone, which would hardly be a better situation. The other thing to remember is that the relationship between your nanny and your child is the first of many similar relationships with people beyond you that your child is going to experience. Relationships with kindergarten teachers, school teachers, sports coaches and music teachers – any of these could create a strong bond, and in such cases you would be wise to be thankful for that.

Dealing with the nanny moving on

My father used to be fond of the expression, 'She was a good cook as far as good cooks go, and as good cooks go, she went'. In other words, all good things come to an end. Unfortunately, when it comes time for your wonderful nanny to move on, it can be an emotional time for all involved.

The typical situation for 'making the break' is at the end of February, when the youngest child has settled into full days at school. The nanny can then potentially return a month or so later, now as a friend rather than a carer. This can be a great way to reassure the children that the nanny is still a friend – that she still loves the kids – while signalling that the relationship has changed.

Of course it isn't always like that, and there can be unhappy 'break ups' (though these are rarely anything to do with the children, most often due to disagreements between mother and nanny). Sometimes the nanny needs to leave for her own reasons, which can leave the parents disgruntled.

Whatever the reason, we come back to the point that the children's welfare needs to come first and, in almost every case, that means that there needs to be an opportunity for the children to say goodbye. We should never forget that, for the children, the nanny is one more person who cares for them and loves them, and so the feelings of the child in this 'separation' need to be acknowledged. There are lots of ways to keep in touch, of course, but I've always felt the best approach is for the nanny to 'fade' out of children's lives gradually. That might mean that she makes a phone call after a month or so, sends a card a few months later and after that sends an ongoing birthday and/or Christmas card.

There also needs to be acknowledgement all along that the nanny is not a permanent part of the family. Dependence needs to be limited and any family needs to understand that they can, and will, get along quite well without their nanny once they make the adjustment.

6
REFLECTIONS ON OUR AGENCY

I'd like to finish this book with some commentary on my agency, Placement Solutions, based in Kew East, Melbourne. I genuinely believe we have built an agency that offers parents the best nannies and nannies the best jobs and support. I would welcome more agencies coming to the fore and challenging us on these measures, but unfortunately too many players in this industry are still concerned with cutting corners, turning over placement assignments and making money. In all of that neither the children, the clients nor the nannies come first.

Why we insist on face-to-face interviews with all our applicants

In the previous chapter I wrote about the things clients need to bear in mind when hiring a nanny. Here I want to share the process we follow when recruiting nannies. The thoroughness of our approach — particularly in insisting on a face-to-face interview — is one of the aspects of our service that we believe makes us stand out from other agencies.

After advertising, we start our process with a telephone screening, mainly as a check that a potential nanny meets our most basic requirements: that they are over 18 and have at least three years of industry experience.

At this point we're also looking to ascertain whether a candidate is serious about the job. Are they currently working? Are they looking for a permanent position or just casual work? What we want to know is whether the person we are talking to is serious about in-home child care as a profession – that they don't see nannying as a fill in between 'real' jobs.

Those who progress past this initial screening are scheduled for a face-to-face interview. We ask them to complete our specially designed application form and present us with their original documentation.

We don't employ any nannies without an interview. In all my years in this business I have always taken this approach. It might be more work – it is certainly time consuming – but it is an investment in making good decisions. Without doing this – and many agencies don't – it is simply not possible to properly understand where someone is coming from, what motivates them and how serious they are about their profession.

In our interviews we are looking for all sorts of things, but most of all for what I call a 'spark'. That spark is hard to pin down, but it consists, I think, of a combination of attitude, passion and professionalism.

Our open-ended interview questions – we see the interview as more of a discussion really – aim at building up a picture of this person, their career so far and their aspirations. We need to be convinced that the potential nanny really wants to keep working with children – that this is something she loves to do. We want to see a desire to be a great, not just good, nanny. We are looking for good communication skills: people who will be equally comfortable communicating with the parents they are working for, with us as their agency, and of course with the children they will be caring for.

Sometimes simply asking an interviewee to tell us about a 'typical day with a three-year-old' will go a long way towards satisfying us (or not) on these things. It's questions like this, and similar behavioural-type questions, that yield so much more information about a candidate than we could ever glean over the phone.

Something else we are looking for is a genuine desire to work with us. Some nannies would prefer to work (illegally) on a cash-in-hand basis – these people won't be employed by our agency. The nannies who do join us understand the benefits of working for a supportive agency, of being paid above-award wages and, importantly, of being offered opportunities for professional development. Again, it is about seeing in-home child care as a profession, not just a job.

After our interviews we do a thorough reference check on shortlisted candidates. These checks allow us to verify claims about experience as well as confirming the sense of the 'person' we got from our interview.

Of an original group of around 40 applicants, we would typically interview nine and employ perhaps five or six. Experience tells us that if we follow our process thoroughly – the telephone screening, face-to-face interview and reference checks – we can be confident that a person we decide to hire is a high-quality nanny who we can trust to look after the children of one of our clients. For this reason we do not take any short cuts in our recruitment process. It is too important to get it right.

The question of fees

The cost of child care is never far from the news, and the cost of in-home child care using a professional nanny is never far from our ears. Questions about the level of our fees are not constant, but they aren't uncommon either – particularly when some of our competitors are offering sometimes significantly lower rates.

So let's pull this fee question apart.

Quality child care is expensive. There is no denying that, and we fully understand that for many people the cost can be onerous. However, we make no apologies for the fact that we choose to offer a premium, full bricks-and-mortar agency service and, as such, our fees are higher than many of the alternatives. We also choose to pay our nannies a reasonable wage. At a recent International Women's Day event the MC asked the audience who was paying for child care and who was paying at the correct rate. Her point was that charity begins at home and working women can't expect to climb to the top on the backs of others.

All women deserve to be paid legally and receive their full entitlements. That is precisely our approach.

There are a number of factors that contribute to the way childcare fees are calculated, both by Placement Solutions and by other providers. The first and most important is staffing costs, by far the largest cost item in any form of child care. Staffing costs depend on two main things: the carer–child ratio and staff on-costs.

On the ratio, the fee implications are simple: the more children each carer looks after, the lower the staffing cost per child. Childcare centres operate with carer–child ratios from one to four (for babies) up to one to 10 (for preschoolers). Family day care and occasional care operate at similar ratios; after-school care usually involves a much higher number of children for each staff member.

Our general approach is to use a ratio of one nanny to one or two children (of any age), with four children as an absolute maximum in special circumstances and with children aged two and up. A nanny earns the same hourly rate and entitlements whether she cares for one child or four, which makes one-on-one care the most costly form of child care available. However the benefits of this are fairly obvious: much greater care and attention given to the child, on top of other benefits of in-home care such as children being happy and comfortable in their own home, with their own toys, gardens and food.

When it comes to on-costs, our philosophy is that we want to attract – and retain – the best nannies we can find in order to provide continuity of outstanding care to our clients and their children. This starts with a thorough recruiting process (as described above), reference and experience checking and confirmation of visa and employment status. We then pay above-award wages at all levels, and reward loyalty and qualifications with higher wages, at three levels, over time.

We provide security to our carers by employing all our nannies directly, rather than as contractors, but this means we need to incorporate superannuation, workers compensation and insurance into our costing structures. We never pay any nanny cash in hand, nor place any nanny as a contractor with her own ABN. These approaches may be cheaper, but they are also illegal under Australian law. This is something you should check if talking to another service.

We also provide regular ongoing professional development to our carers and the support of our permanently staffed office at all times. This support is, of course, also available to our clients.

In short, we provide the very best employment opportunities to our nannies and in turn the very best level of care available for our clients' children. I am confident you will not find an equivalent level of service anywhere else in Victoria, and certainly not for a lower price.

Yes, we could cut costs and provide a more budget-oriented level of care, but that's simply not what we do. What we do is find ways to minimise the impact of fees on our clients, most notably through our accreditation to offer government-subsidised care to eligible families. We always encourage our clients to check their eligibility for these benefits by calling us, Centrelink or the federal Department of Human Services.

We also offer a nanny sharing service, which I'll describe in the next section.

Finding other ways to care

One of the most common comments made about our industry is that hiring a nanny is 'only for the rich'. It is something we are always aware of and looking to improve.

It is inevitable that using a qualified and properly vetted nanny is going to be more expensive than using a childcare centre, if for no other reason than that the ratio of carer to children (usually one to one or one to two for nannies, compared with one to five or more in a centre). One way that we can improve this situation is by facilitating a shared nanny arrangement. It is possible to share a nanny in many circumstances, and it is a great way to get access to all the wonderful things that in-home childcare can provide, for a fraction of the cost. Nanny sharing has the extra bonus of providing extra socialisation for the children involved.

The way we operate nanny sharing is quite simple. It involves one nanny caring for the children of two families at once, up to four children in total. (Our ratio of one to four precludes more than four children being cared for in this way.)

In practice, nanny sharing works by all the children gathering in one of their homes. Most often the home used alternates between the two families in some pattern – it can be daily, or week-about, or whatever works. To keep it simple for our clients, we invoice each family separately, incorporating for each any government assistance or rebates that may apply. (It doesn't matter if one family qualifies for assistance and the other doesn't – the benefit is just applied to the proportion paid by the qualifying family – though eligible clients must be approved to use nanny sharing by the Department of Education.)

Other than that, all aspects of care are handled jointly. At the start, we interview parents from both families together, and we select potential nannies based on the families' joint needs. Later, client liaison visits are also held jointly, which presents an opportunity for any issues – including between families – to be ironed out quickly.

Before considering nanny sharing, there are some things that need to be thought about. In particular, you and your potential 'share parents' need to make sure that you are at one on matters of discipline, nutrition (e.g. sugar 'allowances'), education (e.g. reading expectations) and screen time (TV, devices and games – and what can and cannot be watched or played on them). Nanny sharing simply won't work if there is one set of rules for the children of one family and a different set of rules for the other.

Where these things are in sync, and the two homes aren't too far apart, nanny sharing between two families can be a realistic and money-saving option well worth considering.[4]

• • •

---

[4] Our agency recently released an app to facilitate finding 'matches' for sharing – new technology is perfect for making this task easier.

Something else we introduced as a way of providing more affordable in-home care are our baby care packages. Having your first baby is one of those rare things in life that nothing can properly prepare you for. Many about-to-be parents think that they're on top of it – they've read all the books and listened to all the advice – but when the big day comes and harsh reality sets in, well, let's just say reality turns out to be a lot harder to deal with than theory. It's amazing how something as small as a newborn child can cause so much disruption to your life.

I've already discussed how, on one level, today's new mother has a lot more resources at her disposal than her mother or grandmother before her. On the other hand, today's new mum is also, often, back at home within a day or two of her baby's arrival, and back at work a few weeks after that. Also, changing lifestyles mean that a lot of mothers don't have the hands-on support of a mother or mother-in-law, as they live in another state or work full time themselves.

It was with these things in mind that we started putting together a range of gift packages aimed at helping busy new mothers better prepare for, then survive, the arrival of their first baby. Uniquely, we wanted these packages to include real, in-home assistance from a newborn care specialist at night, giving new mums the chance to get some meaningful sleep – usually one of the biggest struggles of those first few weeks, and something that can make an enormous difference to getting on top of the new routine.

We created baby care packages at various levels, each including the services of one of our newborn care specialists, who fully attends to the new baby's needs between 11 pm and 7 am for two to four nights a week minimum, for up to four weeks. That includes settling, nappy changes and feeding (or bringing baby to mum for feeding). These boxes make delightful and useful gifts and are really appreciated by new parents – more than another bunch of flowers.

The aim of this service is really to provide new parents with some peace of mind – a brief respite in those first crazy weeks. We find that the nanny not only provides hands-on care, but is also able to play an important educational role at a time when many parents can become concerned by the slightest 'strange' behaviour of their baby.

• • •

There is almost no such thing as a 'normal' work pattern or family arrangement anymore. Our industry – and I include government in this, in so far as it is an important provider of funded care – needs to acknowledge this and be looking for new ways of providing care when and where it is needed.

Recognising achievement

I wrote at some length earlier about the need to build a sense of professionalism in the nanny industry, and how that is being achieved in the US in various ways. Unfortunately there has not been the same level of drive from agencies in Australia, collectively, to increase the status of nannies and to recognise achievements in the sector.

This was why, in 2014, my agency decided to take things into our own hands and introduce an Australian Nanny of the Year award that would recognise the personal achievements of a working nanny. I believe it is important that outstanding nannies are recognised not only for the important job they do, and for their personal commitment and skill, but also to reinforce the depth of the role of a nanny in in-home child care.

Initially awarded biennially and with a focus on our own nannies (though open to all past and present employees), our hope is that over time the award and, more importantly its winners, might gain broader recognition within the nanny industry across Australia. Thankfully we were able to link the local Australian award with its US counterpart presented by the INA – an award that has been running for over 30 years and for which Australian winners are encouraged to apply.

I was very pleased to be able to present the inaugural Placement Solutions Australian Nanny of the Year award to Clare Carlisle Stranger in December 2014. Clare had been working as one of our nannies since beginning her career five years earlier.

One of the contributors to Clare's success was the life experience she had before becoming a nanny. She is the mother of two teenage girls and has also worked as a volunteer supporting mothers with postnatal depression. Beyond that, she has a genuine and deep love of children and is an open and honest communicator with the parents whose children she cares for.

In Clare's case, her role as a nanny involves caring for a seven-year-old girl and a nine-year-old boy when they are not at school. Their mother is wheelchair bound and works from home, which creates a more complex dynamic than is often the case. One of Clare's particular skills before the children started school was her ability to successfully manage the situation in a way that allowed her client to get on with her work without needing to create overly rigid barriers between the children and their mother.

Our second winner, in 2016, was Cecily Laing. To say that Cecily is an enthusiast for nannying as a profession would be a gross understatement. She has been a career nanny for as long as she has been working, she loves her job, and she wants to make sure that as many people as possible understand that nannying is a real job and a real career.

Cecily found herself working as a nanny soon after she finished school. She knew she wanted to work with children, but wasn't overly keen on the idea of working with large groups of kids. She counts herself very lucky that, given she had no experience and no qualification, she was trusted by a single mother to care for her infant son. That first employer worked in the film industry so the job was live-in, involved some very odd hours and also involved some travel. Cecily loved every minute.

Cecily has worked as a full-time nanny ever since that first job, in a wide range of capacities that I summarised in Chapter 4.

I've been very pleased that both of our winners have become strong advocates for the nanny industry. As Clare put it:

> I hope that awards such as this assist the whole industry and reinforce the message that a nanny makes an invaluable contribution to the education of the nation's children. It is such an important job and often underestimated – it is far more involved than just 'babysitting'. A good nanny provides a key developmental influence in the life of a child. It is a rewarding and fulfilling career.

Cecily similarly committed to using her position to advocate for her profession at every opportunity:

> I want to bring a positive face to the industry. The only time nannies ever make the news is for bad stuff. 'The nanny did this, the nanny did that.' It would be really good to see some positive stories about nannies doing amazing work.

She is also concerned about preconceptions that nannies are effectively raising children for wealthy parents, as opposed to the reality, in which nannies are very much part of a team, with the parents, that is raising the children together.

The introduction of a Nanny of the Year award in Australia was a long time coming, but I'm really looking forward to recognising more outstanding nannies in the coming years.

Taking the lead on issues that matter

In 1994 I found myself involved in a campaign to introduce mandatory fencing around all swimming pools in Victoria, working at the time with then state Opposition leader John Brumby. This subsequently led to my working to introduce a Working with Children Check in Victoria. I guess I've always felt comfortable taking the lead on issues that matter. Someone has to!

So it was that on 9 August 2014, a few steps ahead of the Victorian government and the rest of our industry, Placement Solutions launched our own Child Protection Policy. We were, as far as I am aware, the first agency of our kind in Australia to document such a policy, and I believe we remain so. Our policy was certainly the first of its kind to be approved by Child Wise, one of Australia's leading not-for-profit child sexual abuse prevention organisations. (Our agency is now Child Wise accredited.)

This didn't happen without a huge amount of work beforehand. We were lucky to have working with us on the policy a lawyer with experience in child protection, who later worked with the Royal Commission into Institutional Responses to Child Sexual Abuse.

Why did we need to go through all this? In our view there is simply not enough child protection provided by the current laws and regulations covering in-home care. For instance, at the time Victorian law did not mandate nannies to report child abuse or the indicators of it. (Thankfully this has since changed.)

Our belief is that adults – parents, carers or otherwise – have a moral and ethical responsibility to keep children safe and protect them from harm, including, of course, physical or emotional abuse. We endeavour to always consider and act in 'the best interests of the child', as outlined in the United Nations Convention on the Rights of the Child, and it is this principle that has driven, and formed the basis of, our policy.

Of course a policy isn't much use unless it can be put into practice, so with this in mind we provide training to all our staff and nannies on its implementation. What this means, first and foremost, when it comes to child abuse is knowing what to look for.

Child abuse is statistically broken up into four areas: sexual abuse, emotional abuse (including bullying), physical abuse and neglect. While sexual and physical abuse tend to get most of the media attention, emotional abuse and neglect can be equally serious. It goes without saying that many instances of abuse involve more than one of these.

I recall learning some challenging statistics in our initial training, including that 94 per cent of all abusers are men. However, when a woman does abuse, the situation tends to be serious. The vast majority (95 per cent) of abusers are known to and trusted by the child. And, while it may seem obvious, it is worth reminding ourselves that abusers don't look different to anybody else.

Our policy document is comprehensive, outlining everything from child abuse indicators to legislative and legal requirements on those reporting abuse, and what to do, and not do, in response to an allegation. We include a step-by-step guide to reporting and a code of conduct.

This policy is now central to our operation and is reviewed annually.

Continued growth

In recent years we have launched two new businesses to sit alongside Placement Solutions. Each plays its role in our drive to improve nanny education and promote the legal employment of nannies.

Nurture Training College RTO (Registered Training Organisation) is our very own college, established to offer the Diploma of Early Childhood Education and Care (formerly the Diploma of Children's Services) and other formal, accredited training relevant to nannies.

The college means we can offer nationally recognised training specifically geared towards the role of the nanny – something that has really not been available to date. The way this works is that we are able to work within the scope of the course guidelines while tailoring our program to the nanny industry. We can also offer flexible delivery options that suit most nannies, such as providing classes on Saturdays and after work hours. At the same time, those undertaking the course will find that it is broadly applicable to (and, importantly, recognised by) the childcare industry.

Another benefit of this particular program, being attached as it is to a nanny agency, is the potential for job placement at the end of the course.

We now have an RTO Manager who is tasked with continuing to establish our diploma course and various short course education programs.

We accept applications to our Diploma of Early Childhood Education and Care program from currently working nannies (whether registered with us or not), those aspiring to be nannies and all those potentially wishing to gain entry into this field of employment. There is no academic prerequisite for the course and applicants only need to complete a short literacy and numeracy assessment to qualify.

Our other new business is Just Family Nanny Payroll. This initiative is all about sharing our existing administrative systems for paying nannies with others who would like to use them rather than build their own from the ground up.

With Just Family Nanny Payroll, parents who want to directly employ a nanny but don't want the hassle of managing their pay, superannuation and so on can have us handle all the bureaucracy for them.

Other potential users of this service are small nanny agencies, anywhere in Australia, that either don't have a complete payroll system themselves or have clients who would prefer to employ their nanny directly.

• • •

As these businesses establish themselves, we will continue to look for new ideas that will help us increase the professionalism of nannies, improve the conditions under which nannies work and, above all else, put the needs of children first.

THE FINAL WORD

This book has been written from the heart but also with a sense of outrage. I have a strong view that while there have been improvements in childcare services over the last 30 years, those of us in this sector can still do so much better.

Our mantra must be to put children first – always. It should be that simple. Everyone in this industry should be striving for honesty and integrity in all that we do, and towards those we care for.

This is a plea not only to those providing services but also to our 'consumers'. In particular, to those parents who associate in-home child care with finding the cheapest hourly rate they can get; who see the care of their children as no more than 'sitting'; who expect that their nanny should be doing household chores like cleaning in the thirty minutes that their child naps. Would these parents expect a neurosurgeon to swab the floor between brain operations? Would you expect a lawyer to put on an apron and cook the judges' lunch?

Nannies, as I've been at pains to emphasise throughout this book, are professionals. Their job involves being 100 per cent present and in the moment for the children they are looking after. Children rely on this active presence and engagement: it's how young humans learn and develop. They rely on all their carers to be hyper-vigilant, enthusiastic and, above all, kind.

Honesty and integrity must extend to agencies as well. There is no place in the childcare industry for agencies that are driven by profit alone and that therefore short-change parents, children and the nannies they represent to make an extra dollar. To those who run these agencies I ask, are you otherwise upright citizens who obey the laws, who opt to pay for the goods and services you buy? I'm sure you are. So why, then, do you believe it is okay to deny employment benefits to the nannies you represent? To deny them workers compensation insurance, superannuation and/or social security? Why do you believe it is okay not to train and develop, encourage and professionalise your nannies?

Lastly, to those bureaucrats and politicians who devise and implement policies in this area, my request is simple. Please sit down and talk to the experienced in this field. Stop trivialising the role of the professional nanny by calling us 'babysitters' and by turning a blind eye to those who flout employment and tax laws when employing nannies.

Our children are precious. Let's not forget that they are the reason we do what we do.

About the author

Louise Dunham is the CEO of Placement Solutions, a Melbourne-based niche recruitment firm specialising in the placement of nannies and household organisers. Louise established this business in 1988.

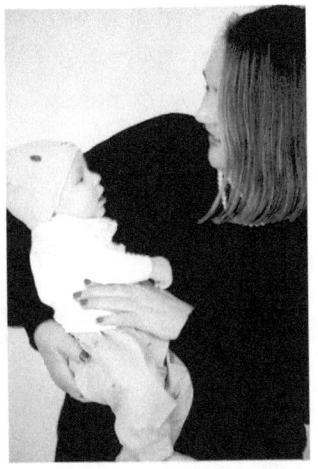

Louise served on the National Steering Committee that wrote the Interim In-Home Care Standards that are used to set quality guidelines within the in-home childcare sector. She is a passionate advocate for the need for nannies to be developed and recognised as childcare professionals and to be legally paid and supported as having a valuable role to play within the greater childcare sector.

In 2012, Louise attained a board position with the USA-based

International Nanny Association (INA), the first non-American to take such a position in its then 31-year history. She served as chair of the INA's Ethics Committee from 2012 until 2017 and also served as the association's vice president.

Louise has also been a vice president on the board of the Australian Home Childcare Association (AHCA), the peak body for the in-home childcare sector in Australia, overseeing the marketing and public relations functions.

In addition to establishing Placement Solutions, Louise has also set up Just Family Nanny Payroll Services (catering for both her regular clients and other clients who self-employ a nanny but choose to outsource their payroll and other legal administrative responsibilities) and Nurture Training College an RTO (providing formal qualifications in the nationally accredited Diploma and Certificate 3 in Early Childhood Education and Care and nanny specific short courses and electives).

Louise is a former high school english and history teacher. She spends her spare time delving into family history, writing, gardening and being a granny nanny to her grandson.

Me and my mother at my grandparents' home in Christchurch, New Zealand – late 1954.

Mum and me at a birthday party at home in Ulverstone, Tasmania – circa 1955.

Me, Sianan and Caitlin at my parents' home in Launceston, Tasmania – 1991.

My daughters Sianan and Caitlin outside Placement Solutions first office in Ivanhoe, Victoria – 1995.

Scout, great niece, and me – circa 2011.

Caitlin, me and newborn grandson Reuben – August 2015.

Family at our stall at the Pregnancy Babies and Children's Expo – 2016.

www.ingramcontent.com/pod-product-compliance
Lightning Source LLC
Chambersburg PA
CBHW021128300426
44113CB00006B/341